The Uncertain Web

Rob Larsen

T0256853

Beijing · Cambridge · Farnham · Köln · Sebastopol · Tokyo

The Uncertain Web

by Rob Larsen

Copyright © 2015 Rob Larsen. All rights reserved.

Printed in the United States of America.

Published by O'Reilly Media, Inc., 1005 Gravenstein Highway North, Sebastopol, CA 95472.

O'Reilly books may be purchased for educational, business, or sales promotional use. Online editions are also available for most titles (*http://safaribooksonline.com*). For more information, contact our corporate/institutional sales department: 800-998-9938 or *corporate@oreilly.com*.

Editors: Simon St. Laurent and Amy Jolly-more
Production Editor: Colleen Lobner
Copyeditor: Marta Justak
Proofreader: Jasmine Kwityn

Indexer: Ellen Troutman-Zaig
Cover Designer: Ellie Volckhausen
Interior Designer: David Futato
Illustrator: Rebecca Demarest

December 2014:   First Edition

Revision History for the First Edition:

2014-12-02:   First release

2015-01-07:   Second release

See *http://oreilly.com/catalog/errata.csp?isbn=9781491945902* for release details.

ISBN: 978-1-491-94590-2

[LSI]

Table of Contents

Preface

The best way to approach the Web today is to forgo hard-and-fast rules and design for uncertainty. Embracing uncertainty as a core tenet of web development and scrapping the rules we've relied on in the past few years is the best bet for creating future-proof web solutions.

In the early 2000s, there was basically one browser (Internet Explorer 6), one platform (Windows XP), and one screen resolution (1024 × 768) that mattered. With that setup, you could design, develop, and test the vast majority of web users with one desktop computer. The biggest question on the horizon, it seemed, was when it would be viable to design for 1280-pixel screens.

This limited field of play meant that there was an expectation that sites and applications would look the same everywhere for everyone. Best practices were honed and codified into hard-and-fast rules that drove design and development. Major choices, such as the size of the basic design grid, were no longer *choices*. Everyone started with a static, 960-pixel grid and then sliced and diced it as needed.

Today, things couldn't be more different. With the launch of the iPhone and the iPad, the rise of Android, and the growth of not just one but two real contenders to Microsoft's position as the dominant desktop web browser (Firefox and Chrome), developers and designers have an ocean of variables to navigate. Every question around a site design is now filled with options.

Initially, developers and designers tried to navigate this new reality by creating new rules. But the problem was that the goalposts kept moving. As soon as a new hard and fast rule was created, some new wrinkle would render it impotent. People designed and built iPhone sites, assuming that Apple's dominance in the smartphone market was a permanent condition. They tested for touch capabilities and assumed that touch users would never have a mouse.

As Android's huge growth over the past few years, and the presence of Chromebooks and Windows 8 laptops with both mouse and touch capabilities have proved, those new rules have a short shelf life.

Even patterns like responsive web design (RWD), which some saw as a single solution for design and development moving forward, fell apart when applied against complicated application patterns and the questions of bandwidth and the challenge of mobile performance.

By combining web standards, progressive enhancement, an iterative approach to design and development, and a desire to question the status quo, teams can create sites and applications that should perform well in a wide range of present and future devices. By focusing on optimal solutions with intelligent fallbacks and forgoing the desire for absolute solutions, design and development can work together to create a Web that is fast, widely available, and reliable.

This book will outline both the concept and underlying principles of the uncertain Web and introduce some of the techniques necessary to make the successful transition.

A Word on the Web Today

The evolution of the Web as a development platform and the incredible growth in the number of web-enabled devices has pushed the Web into places it could never have reached before. In the past decade, we've gone from a stagnant platform with a handful of browsers and operating systems connecting to the Web to a vibrant, Open Web Platform serving a dizzying array of browsers and devices.

That's the big picture.

The thing is, most of the time, front-line developers don't get to spend time looking at the big picture. You know how it is—it's usually a challenge just getting the next release out the door. Whether you're building a site for a client, working on the latest version of your JavaScript framework, or simply trying to make sure people can read the text on your blog, there's not a lot of time available to muse about the way the Web as a whole has changed. Instead, you focus on solutions to individual problems, because those are the ones keeping you from going home at a reasonable hour. Even folks who are tasked with keeping track of the big trends can get sidetracked by specific storms that pop up. It's hard to keep your eye on the big picture when you're watching 10 (long!) emails an hour come through on a standards topic you're following with interest.

That's where this book comes in. Judging by the conversations I see on GitHub, StackOverflow, Twitter, and IRC, it seems like people don't really think about how fundamentally the Web has changed. Whether it's searching for the perfect test to detect a "mouse" user versus a "touch" user or designing a responsive site for the "perfect" set of media query breakpoints, there are many developers still trying to hammer out absolute rules and rigid best practices. People are clearly looking to develop sites and applications within clearly defined boundaries.

Although that can be a comforting idea and was once possible, those days are long gone. It's time for a new approach.

The quote from Yehuda Katz at the beginning of the first chapter, sums up, cleverly, two of the threads that you'll see throughout the book. Flip ahead and check it out, or read it live on Twitter (*http://bit.ly/uw-katz*).

Hopefully, when you're done with this book, you'll be doing less crying.

Today's Web is a wild place. The Web has *never* been a static platform, no matter how much people might wish it were so. You just can't control who's going to request your content. You can't control the browser or device they're using, and you certainly can't guarantee things like the operating system, screen resolution, bandwidth, or available system fonts. For developers coming from pretty much any other discipline, the number of things that are out of the developer's control can be mind-boggling. That statement will only grow more true with every passing day. Standards are changing on, in some cases, a daily or weekly basis, new devices are coming online at a furious pace, and browser vendors are going at it tooth and nail to innovate their way to the top of the league tables. With an ecosystem like that, trying to collapse everything you do as a developer into something that can fit into a neat little box is a recipe for frustration. Embracing the ecosystem for the wild mess that it is and developing with an eye toward the uncertainty the Web will throw at you is the best way to reach whomever might want to get at your site or application with whatever they have in their pocket or on their desktop—now and in the future.

The tools to do this are already here; you just need an adjustment in the way you view the Web and the way you develop for it.

Who Should Read This Book

The primary audience is intermediate to advanced web developers—the folks on the front lines of dealing with these issues on a day-to-day basis and those who serve as the main channel for new frontend development techniques and trends to make their way into organizations. This book is geared toward developers who work primarily in HTML, CSS, and JavaScript and who have a solid understanding of cross-browser (if not cross-form-factor or cross-device) development techniques.

The secondary audience consists of user experience designers, web-focused visual designers, and web-focused engineers from other programming disciplines. To properly build for the modern Web, there needs to be cohesion in site design and architecture from start to finish. The material here should familiarize other disciplines with the best way to approach designing and developing for the present and future of the Web. As a natural bridge between design and the server, the core web developer is always going to be the glue that binds this process together, but having everyone on board will help improve the finished product.

Navigating This Book

This book is organized into three parts.

Chapter 1 and Chapter 2 will establish the current environment we're in and show us how embracing uncertainty and building for the Web as it exists is the way to go. If you've been handed this book by a coworker and you're not particularly technical (at least in terms of frontend development), then these two chapters (and the conclusion) are the ones to read.

The next several chapters present some of the technical challenges we're facing on the Web and illustrate some of the ways that embracing uncertainty can help solve them. Chapter 3 provides a quick introduction to Modernizr and feature detection (techniques to enable or disable functionality based on browser support). From there, we move on to responsive web design (Chapter 4), user input in the current multidevice landscape (Chapter 5), images on the Web (Chapter 6), and modern web video (Chapter 7). If you're interested in a way to think about this stuff technically, then you'll want to read these chapters. Each one is split between examining the true scope of a problem on the modern Web and looking at solutions and how embracing uncertainty can help you reach the widest possible audience.

I didn't plan it this way when I started the book, but the last three technical chapters (Chapters 5–7) represent the full spectrum of success and failure in the standards process. Video represents a good standard gone bad, user input represents a problem still in search of a solution after several years of development, and images represent a success created by the entire technical web community (standards authors, web developers, and browser vendors).

Chapter 8 takes a final look at the uncertain Web and then talks about the Web as I want to see it evolve over the next 20 years.

Online Resources

The following sites are where modern web design and development are being figured out. These sites have all directly influenced the development of this book:

- HTML5 Rocks—A resource for Open Web HTML5 developers (*http://www.html5rocks.com/en/*)
- LukeW Ideation + Design | Digital Product Strategy & Design (*http://www.lukew.com/*)
- QuirksMode—for all your browser quirks (*http://www.quirks mode.org/*)
- Web Hypertext Application Technology Working Group (*http://www.whatwg.org/*)
- The Modernizr issue tracker on GitHub (*https://github.com/Modernizr/Modernizr/issues?state=open*)
- CSS Tricks (*http://css-tricks.com/*)
- A List Apart: For People Who Make Websites (*http://alista part.com/*)

Conventions Used in This Book

The following typographical conventions are used in this book:

Italic

> Indicates new terms, URLs, email addresses, filenames, and file extensions.

`Constant width`

> Used for program listings, as well as within paragraphs to refer to program elements such as variable or function names, databases, data types, environment variables, statements, and keywords.

`Constant width bold`

> Shows commands or other text that should be typed literally by the user.

`Constant width italic`

> Shows text that should be replaced with user-supplied values or by values determined by context.

 This icon signifies a tip, suggestion, or general note.

 This icon indicates a warning or caution.

Using Code Examples

Supplemental material (code examples, exercises, etc.) is available for download at *https://github.com/roblarsen/the-uncertain-web*.

This book is here to help you get your job done. In general, if example code is offered with this book, you may use it in your programs and documentation. You do not need to contact us for permission unless you're reproducing a significant portion of the code. For example, writing a program that uses several chunks of code from this book does not require permission. Selling or distributing a CD-ROM of examples from O'Reilly books does require permission. Answering a question by citing this book and quoting example code does not require permission. Incorporating a significant amount of example code from this book into your product's documentation does require permission.

We appreciate, but do not require, attribution. An attribution usually includes the title, author, publisher, and ISBN. For example: "*The Uncertain Web* by Rob Larsen (O'Reilly). Copyright 2015 Rob Larsen, 978-1-491-94590-2."

If you feel your use of code examples falls outside fair use or the permission given above, feel free to contact us at *permissions@oreilly.com*.

Safari® Books Online

 *Safari Books Online* is an on-demand digital library that delivers expert content in both book and video form from the world's leading authors in technology and business.

Technology professionals, software developers, web designers, and business and creative professionals use Safari Books Online as their primary resource for research, problem solving, learning, and certification training.

Safari Books Online offers a range of product mixes and pricing programs for organizations, government agencies, and individuals. Subscribers have access to thousands of books, training videos, and prepublication manuscripts in one fully searchable database from publishers like O'Reilly Media, Prentice Hall Professional, Addison-Wesley Professional, Microsoft Press, Sams, Que, Peachpit Press, Focal Press, Cisco Press, John Wiley & Sons, Syngress, Morgan Kaufmann, IBM Redbooks, Packt, Adobe Press, FT Press, Apress, Manning, New Riders, McGraw-Hill, Jones & Bartlett, Course Technology, and dozens more. For more information about Safari Books Online, please visit us online.

How to Contact Us

Please address comments and questions concerning this book to the publisher:

> O'Reilly Media, Inc.
> 1005 Gravenstein Highway North
> Sebastopol, CA 95472
> 800-998-9938 (in the United States or Canada)
> 707-829-0515 (international or local)
> 707-829-0104 (fax)

We have a web page for this book, where we list errata, examples, and any additional information. You can access this page at *http://bit.ly/uncertain_web*.

To comment or ask technical questions about this book, send email to *bookquestions@oreilly.com*.

For more information about our books, courses, conferences, and news, see our website at *http://www.oreilly.com*.

Find us on Facebook: *http://facebook.com/oreilly*

Follow us on Twitter: *http://twitter.com/oreillymedia*

Watch us on YouTube: *http://www.youtube.com/oreillymedia*

Acknowledgments

I'd like to thank all the people who put up with me pestering them for feedback while I was developing this idea into a proper book. In particular, Paul Irish, Bob Holt, Marc Neuwirth, and Adam McIntyre all provided great feedback on the concept and the title. Thanks to you guys, I felt like I was actually onto something. Bob and Adam deserve double thanks for their excellent technical (and beyond) feedback throughout the writing process.

Everyone from O'Reilly has been great throughout this project, and I want to wrap the whole company up in a bear hug for that. I especially want to thank Simon St. Laurent for taking an idea sketched out in a few paragraphs and pitched at the airport in Denver and then turning it into the book you're reading now. I also have to thank Amy Jollymore for shepherding me through this project with welcome positivity and great insight.

I'd also like to thank Lynn Haller from Studio B for getting this concept into O'Reilly's hands in the first place and for taking care of the business end of this whole book-writing thing.

Finally, I'd like to thank my wife for her love and support. I'm always busy doing something silly like writing a book, and she's always there for me. I couldn't ask for anything more.

CHAPTER 1
Embracing Uncertainty

The web platform is Write Once, Cry Everywhere.

— Yehuda Katz

I love the Web. I've been making sites for a living since 1999, and I still love the work as much as I did in those crazy days. I'm not sure how many other folks I know who can say the same thing about their profession. Admittedly, the Web has been very good to me. I've been able to travel the world, have written a bunch of articles and a couple of books, and have paid my bills with nothing but a keyboard for the past decade and a half. The thing is, while all that is great and I thank my lucky stars that I've had this career, what I really love about the Web is that it made good on its early promise. It might have sounded a little hokey or looked like just hype to fill a five-minute slot on the evening news, but the Web really has managed to connect people in incredible ways—ways we couldn't even have imagined 25 years ago. Individuals who would never have had a voice can now broadcast to the world with blogs, YouTube, Twitter, and Facebook. Politicians, filmmakers, video game developers, and anyone else with an idea can tap into the power of individuals to finance their dreams, five dollars at a time. Lessons from the world's great universities like Stanford and MIT, as well as lessons made directly for the Web from organizations like Khan Academy, are available for free to anyone in the world who can connect to the Web. With sites like GitHub, taking part in open source software is as easy as firing up a web browser and finding a place to help out with even the most massive open source projects like jQuery, Node.js, or Ruby on Rails.

It's only getting better. As more and more people come online, they're exposed to these same opportunities and start to feed back into the system with a unique voice: hard work on some open source bug, adding to the coverage of breaking news (say, sharing a photo of a plane landing on the Hudson River (*http://bit.ly/uw-plane*)), or something as simple as buying a business cat tie on Etsy (*http://bit.ly/uw-cat-tie*) and turning the wheels of commerce.

It's really pretty cool.

I could go on about this for a while and, if I didn't have other plans, I'd be tempted to do just that. I *do* have plans though, so I'm going to resist the impulse.

This chapter will introduce the core concept of uncertainty in the context of web development. From there, we'll look at where we came from with Microsoft's monoculture in the early 2000s, and then we'll look in depth at where we are today. Throughout, we'll look at what the factors that have gotten us here can teach us about the future of the Open Web Platform and related ecosystem.

You won't be an absolute expert on everything the Web has to offer just by reading this chapter, but you should have a much better sense of where we've been, where we are, what's on the horizon, what some current issues are, and what kinds of things might surprise us in the future.

Embrace Uncertainty

Along with the landscape, the general philosophy of making websites and applications has slowly shifted over the past decade or so. It's moved gradually from the rigorously defined boundaries of the Microsoft monoculture to the fluid environment we have today. Design approaches like responsive web design, technology patterns like progressive enhancement, and libraries like Modernizr are all much better suited to today's Web than anything that came before. Fixed-width sites with "best viewed with" banners that broke without third-party plug-ins like Adobe Flash or failed to function if the user visited with a new, novel web browser (no matter how powerful) don't have to exist anymore. We're better than that.

That's a good start.

The thing is, although we've mostly shifted away from static 960px grids and all of the other baggage that came with the limited universe, the shift has been isolated to islands of innovation and has generally only happened in reaction to outside stimuli. Every change in the browser and device landscape has sent people scurrying, trying to solve problems caused by new features, browsers, or form factors. Although there have been some truly flexible solutions crafted for these issues, there are just as likely to be a newly revised set of inflexible guidelines put up, only to be revisited the next time the landscape shifts. It's time to get ahead of the curve and do our best to cure the disease and not just treat the symptoms.

It's time to embrace uncertainty.

Embracing uncertainty means that we need to make the final leap away from the search for absolutes in order to appreciate the Web for what it actually is. As we'll examine in this chapter, it's a place where a wide range of devices running a wide range of web browsers in the hands of many different kinds of people are all trying to find their way to something that matters to them. Whether it's a farmer in Africa trying to figure out the score of the latest Manchester United match, a banker in Hong Kong trying to get a price for Bordeaux futures, or a small business owner in the United States setting up an Etsy shop, the Web is making important connections for people, and we need to help them on their way.

So how to do it?

We'll start by looking at specific recommendations beginning with the next chapter, but even before you start to look at the particulars, you can start to change the way you look at the process.

The initial step is to understand, from the second that you start a site design, that you (*probably*) can't control what devices, browsers, and form factors will be ingesting your content. Even better, if you can let go of the *desire* to control what devices, browsers, and form factors are accessing your site, you'll be even happier with your results. While some organizations and certain applications *can* dictate specific browser and OS versions, you're probably not going to be able to do so on your end. Unless you're in control of your users' machines or are offering something no one can get anywhere else, you should be trying to satisfy as many browsers and devices as you possibly can.

"But My Client Doesn't Care"

A common issue when people start to embrace anything new in the web development sphere, whether it's a formal usability program, an accessibility initiative, or a web performance optimization project, is getting buy-in from clients or internal stakeholders who might not immediately understand the benefit of something new and unfamiliar. I imagine much the same reaction to the concepts present in this book. I've certainly seen my share of pushback when sharing some of the ideas I'll be discussing, so I expect other people will see the same thing. All you can do is do what I've done: make your case with enthusiasm and data to back it up. You can't force people to change their ways, but if you present good data with conviction, you've got a better chance than if you sit idly by and do nothing.

The next, most important step is not only to accept that you can't control the browser and device environment, but to embrace the ecosystem for what it is—a sign that the Web is a healthy platform. Tens of thousands of browser/device/OS combinations is a *feature* of the Web, not a problem.

I talk to a lot of people, and there are plenty of complaints about the Web as a platform. I'm not talking about specific complaints about specific features. I'm talking about complaints about the Web itself.

Many Java/C/C++ developers just shake their heads at the idea that code written for the Web can be executed in so many different environments and can have just as many different results. To them, the Web is just nuts. On the other end of the spectrum, many web developers have their favorite browsers, great hardware, new smartphones, and everything else gets the short end of the stick. These are the folks who go over the top in GitHub issues with their hatred of Internet Explorer, test 99% of the time in Chrome, and are actively wishing for WebKit to be the only rendering engine on the Web because it would make things so much easier for them.

Don't be either extreme.

Instead of worrying about the fracture in the Web and wishing that it was something else, accept the Web for the blessing that it is. And it is a blessing. Because the core technology can run, unaltered, on billions of devices in the hands of billions of people, you have immediate access to all of those billions of people and all of those billions of devices.

How great is that?

From Microsoft's Monoculture to Today's Healthy Chaos

In the early 2000s, there was basically one browser, one platform, and one screen resolution that mattered. You could test the experience of the vast majority of your users, with excellent fidelity, simply by running Windows XP with Internet Explorer 6 and switching between a couple of different screen resolutions (i.e., 800 × 600 and 1024 × 768 pixels). Add in Internet Explorer 5 and 5.5, and you could hit, by some estimates, more than 95% of the Web. (*http://bit.ly/uw-browser-share*) In the end, Internet Explorer held market share of near or above 90% for most of the first half of the 2000s.

To Be Fair, Internet Explorer Was the Good Browser in 1999

Whatever you might think of their business practices at the time (and the courts certainly didn't take kindly to them (*http://www.justice.gov/atr/cases/f3800/msjudgex.htm#vf*)), if you had to choose to *develop* for any browser in the late dot-com era, it was going to be Internet Explorer. Far from being the butt of jokes, Internet Explorer versions 4 through 6 were, at the time, each the best available browser by a wide margin. I've said it many times, and I'll say it again here, the worst major browser ever was Netscape 4. Internet Explorer 6 may have overstayed its welcome by about seven years, but Netscape 4 was simply born bad.

What's more, beyond simply being the most powerful browser, the Internet Explorer team consistently pushed out powerful features and APIs that still resonate on the Web today. For one example, the XMLHttpRequest object, which serves as the foundation of modern frontend development, was an Internet Explorer innovation. It really doesn't get any more important than that, in terms of single innovations that have changed the way that we architect web solutions.

For more perspective on what Internet Explorer brought to the Web in those early days, check out my blog post, "Some Internet Explorer Innovations You Probably Forgot About While Waiting for IE6 To Die" (*http://bit.ly/uw-ie-innov*) and Nicholas Zakas' blog post, "The Innovations of Internet Explorer." (*http://bit.ly/uw-ie-innov2*)

Slowly, from the height of Internet Explorer's dominance (reached in the middle of 2004 (*http://bit.ly/uw-ie-dominance*)), things began to turn. It really started with Firefox, the heir to the Netscape mantle, chipping away at Internet Explorer's dominance by presenting an independent, standards-compliant alternative. With Opera revamped for modern development in 2003 (it had previously been great for CSS and *weird* for JavaScript), the 2003 release of Apple Safari, and 2008 release of Google's Chrome browser, Internet Explorer had real competition on multiple fronts, each taking a chunk out of the giant until it was eventually toppled as not only the dominant browser version, but the dominant browser family in May 2012 (*http://bit.ly/uw-chrome-dominance*).

What's more, while all that desktop competition was heating up, an entirely new front in the browser wars opened up with the unprecedented growth of the mobile Web. With the launch of the iPhone and iPad and the dominant growth of phones powered by Google's Android operating system that followed, both the absolute number of users and the number of devices used to connect to the Web per user grew.

Additionally, browser vendors have almost universally (with Apple being the only holdout) instituted a policy automatically pushing updates. Gone are the days of new browser versions shipping every couple of years alongside a new OS update. This new commitment from the browser vendors has allowed us to add new web platform features at a breakneck pace. It has also led to a spread of browser versions, as different organizations and individuals move to the latest version at their own speed.

So, instead of having a couple of machines dedicated to testing and getting 95% coverage, anyone who really pays attention to this stuff can have a testing lab with 50 or more devices and still struggle to cover the same high proportion of the Web that was possible during Microsoft's heyday.

If Hollywood were going to do an edgy reboot of the "Rip Van Winkle" story, they might as well use a web developer, because a developer taking a nap under his desk (as I often threaten to do) in 2004 and waking up today would be bewildered by the changes in the landscape. Imagine a cockeyed Owen Wilson asking, "Google has a browser?" There'd be a lot of that kind of thing.

I mean, I've been paying close attention the whole time, and the changes are just nuts to me.

Let's make some sense of it all.

Where We Are Right Now

I don't think you'd find anyone outside of Redmond who yearns for the days when Internet Explorer was basically the whole Web, though I can't help but think there's a *little* bit of "be careful what you wish for" in the current state of affairs. It wasn't quite as exciting and no-where near as powerful, but it was much easier to wrap your head around the ecosystem in 2003. These days, it's sometimes hard to wrap your head around individual topics. Because it's so complicated, this section is going to focus on making general sense of the current ecosystem.

Plainly stated, the number of variables at play in terms of screen resolution, pixel depth, browser capabilities, form factors, and human–computer interface input options are practically infinite. You can start to tally up the possibilities as we go through the details of the various sections. "Let's see, we've got 10 major browser versions; 50 different screen resolutions between 340px × 280px and 3840px × 1080px; pixel densities in a spectrum from from 72dpi up past 300dpi." Add to that the incredible growth of *new* web-enabled devices and related mobile-driven penetration of previously untapped web markets, like most of Africa, and the idea that you can create any finite set of guidelines and still produce quality web experience for the largest possible audience is pretty much crazy.

On with the show.

Browsers

Every discussion of the state of the web platform begins with the web browser. These days, the browser landscape is robust, with as much competition as we've ever had (see Figure 1-1). They're split across several browser vendors and muliple version numbers, but there are basically four broad streams in the world of browser development. At the heart of each of these streams is a layout engine. For the uninitiated, the layout engine is the core code in a web browser that defines how markup and styles are rendered.

Figure 1-1. Logos from 18 different browsers or browser versions

These streams are as follows:

Microsoft's Trident, which powers Internet Explorer
After twiddling their thumbs for the better part of a decade with Internet Explorer 6 eventually dragging the whole Web down, Microsoft is thankfully back in the business of making good web browsers. Older versions of Internet Explorer (6–8) are still a pox on the Web. IE9 and above are considered "modern browsers," which is shorthand for something that most people are happy to code for. Trident also shows up in other Windows-based applications as a ready-made web browsing component; so if you ever find yourself trying to debug some Windows app that also allows you to browse web pages, try to figure out what version of Trident it's running.

Browsers based on the WebKit open source project
This used to be a larger category (more on that in a second), but it still includes Apple's Safari on the desktop, iOS Safari, older versions of Google's Chrome, the Android Browser, and dozens of other niche browsers, including those running on BlackBerry devices, pre-Microsoft Nokia devices, and the Playstation 3 and 4. For many years, WebKit led the standards charge, and it still will play a strong role in standards efforts going forward.

Browsers based on the Blink open source project
Forked from WebKit in 2013, Blink is the layout engine behind the latest versions of Chrome and Opera. With both companies having a heavy focus on the standards process, Blink might be the gold standard for cutting-edge web development moving forward.

Mozilla's Gecko, which runs under the hood of Firefox
As an independent voice not tied to a large corporate entity (Mozilla is a nonprofit organization), Gecko is both important for

driving standards *and* as an independent foil to the more corporate stakeholders in the development of the web platform

In addition to the rendering engine, each of these streams has an associated JavaScript engine, which completes the core platform functionality for each when packaged as a web browser. These JavaScript Engines are as follows:

Chakra

This is used in Internet Explorer. It is a massive improvement from the engine running in legacy versions of the browser. Interestingly, it compiles scripts on a separate CPU core, parallel to the web browser.

SquirrelFish Extreme/Nitro

It's the JavaScript engine for WebKit.

V8

This is the JavaScript engine used in Google Chrome and Blink-derived versions of Opera. It's also at the core of Node.js, and it is a very influential project. V8 was the first JavaScript engine to compile JavaScript to native code before executing it, increasing performance significantly from previous engines.

SpiderMonkey

It's the JavaScript engine in Firefox. The heir to the original JavaScript engine, it is written by JavaScript's creator Brendan Eich.

These four streams are very competitive on both JavaScript and rendering fronts, which is why working with modern browsers is now *generally* a pretty good experience. And although there are differences between browsers in each stream (both based on when the specific browser version was created and on downstream changes made to the code for specific vendors' needs), knowledge of each stream can serve as a shorthand for what to expect with each browser based on the stream.

Of course, all of these streams break down further into specific browsers. That's where things get really complicated. It's possible to keep track of the various streams, but it's much tougher to deal with specific browser versions.

Depending on your geographical focus or vertical, there are probably 6–10 general browser families you might have to pay attention to on a given project, and each of them might contain two or more specific active versions:

Internet Explorer

Depending on your market, you might have to test against *six* versions of Internet Explorer (6–11). After the dormancy of the mid-2000s, IE is basically releasing a new version every year, allowing for a much faster introduction of new features. Microsoft has also joined the automatic update brigade, which is a welcome change after years of a very conservative update policy.

Firefox

Most people running Firefox are on the automatic upgrade cycle, so it's generally OK to simply test against the latest version, although if you've got an "enterprise" market it might be useful to test against the Extended Support Release (*http://bit.ly/uw-firefox-esr*). Firefox is on a short release cycle, releasing multiple new versions every year.

Chrome

Most people running Chrome on the desktop are automatically updated to the latest version. Chrome pioneered the short browser release cycle.

Safari

Versions 5–8 can be seen in the wild. Major releases are slower than other browsers, although they do bundle features into minor releases.

Opera

Most people running Opera on the desktop are automatically updated to the latest version. Opera is on a rapid release cycle.

Chrome (mobile)

There are mobile versions of Chrome available for iOS and Android 4.0+. In a twist that perfectly sums up how complicated the browser universe is, Chrome for Android uses Blink, and Chrome for iOS uses WebKit. There's also a Samsung-based fork of Chrome that accounts for something like 25% of mobile Chrome traffic. (*http://bit.ly/uw-samsung-chrome*)

iOS Safari

Safari on iOS is updated along with the OS, so you have to look at iOS version numbers to assess what versions are in play. This is iOS 5–8 at its broadest. (iOS 5.1.1 is the highest available for the first-generation iPad.)

Opera Mini

If you don't pay attention to the mobile browser space, it might surprise you how popular this browser is on mobile devices. Data is sent through a proxy server and compressed, saving you time and data. There are a lot of versions of this out there. You will see examples from the 4, 5, and 7* versions in the wild.

Opera Mobile

This is a blink-based browser for Android.

Android Browser

This is the default browser on Android phones. Like iOS Safari, it varies with the Android version and can differ from device to device, because anyone from carriers to device manufacturers has access to the code before it gets into your hand. There could be dozens of different variations out there.

IE Mobile

Based on Trident, versions 9 (appearing on Windows Phone 7), 10 (Windows Phone 8), and 11 (Windows Phone 8.1) are in the wild.

UC Browser

This is a mobile, proxy browser based on the WebKit rendering engine. It's popular in China, India, and other emerging markets.

That's a pretty daunting list. It was only a few years ago that we would point to the Yahoo! Graded Browser Support Table (*http://bit.ly/uw-gbs*) and call it a day. Now you don't want to blink, lest some other entry show up on the back of some new OS or handset.

Before we move on from here, it's worth getting a general sense of the popularity of each of these browsers and of the browser families. You're going to want to make decisions based on *your* needs, but you can't do that without having plenty of information at your disposal.

Let's take a look at a couple of snapshots of the browser market as of March 2014. First, let's look at desktop and tablet browsers with Table 1-1 and the associated bar chart in Figure 1-3. These are good numbers, but are skewed by the fact that StatCounter isn't as strong in some places (e.g., China), as it is in others. That manifests itself most prominently in the absence of IE6 from these charts (it's bundled into "other"), where it should at least gain a mention because it's still a big browser in China. With that caveat aside, it is useful to take a look at the spread across individual browser versions. The biggest negative on the list is probably IE8 still hanging out at 6.2%. I'm sure 360 Safe Browser (*http://www.360safe.com/*) is going to have some of you confused as well. It's a Chinese browser with a publicized security focus (that might actually be loaded with spyware (*http://bit.ly/uw-360-malware*)) based on Trident.

Table 1-1. Desktop browser market share

Browser	Market share %
Chrome (all)	43.66
Firefox 5+	18.27
IE 11.0	8.27
IE 8.0	6.2
Safari iPad	5.19
IE 10.0	3.83
IE 9.0	3.5
Safari 7.0	1.76
Android	1.18
Safari 5.1	1.05
Safari 6.1	0.89
360 Safe Browser 0	0.84
Opera 15+	0.69
Other	4.66

Source: *http://gs.statcounter.com/*

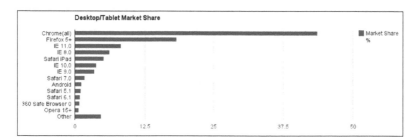

Figure 1-2. Desktop/tablet browser market share

Table 1-2 and the associated bar chart in Figure 1-2 show the mobile market. For many people, the fact that the stock Android browser,

Chrome, and Safari on the iPhone don't make up 100% of the market might come as a shock, but it's true. Unless you're really paying attention, you're probably missing 50% of the mobile browser market in your testing. You're not alone. I asked on Google Plus how many people had ever tested with Opera mobile, and two people said yes. I asked at a table of speakers at a jQuery conference how many had ever heard of UC Browser, and no one had.

Table 1-2. Mobile market share

Browser	Market share %
Android	25.74
iPhone	21.5
Opera	13.03
Chrome	13.59
UC Browser	11.17
Nokia	5.21
IE Mobile	2.19
Other	7.57

Source: *http://gs.statcounter.com/*

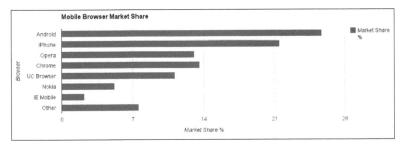

Figure 1-3. Mobile browser market share

It's important to know what's out there, and it's imperative to test against as many of these browsers as possible, but it's rarely useful, when you're sitting down to develop a site, to fixate on the ins and outs of any one particular browser or to target code specifically for certain browsers or browser versions. For starters, it's an overwhelming list, and if you try to fork your code based on every browser and version, you'll end up playing the world's worst game of Whack-a-Mole. Instead, for development, you need to think in terms of features. This concept, *feature detection* (versus *browser detection*) has been a common concept in web development for a long time, but now it's more important than it's ever been. We'll talk more about how to leverage feature detection (and when to make an exception and fall back to browser detection) in Chapter 3, but the core concept is not to ask "What browser is this?" It's to ask "Does your browser support the feature I want to use?"

That will help you if some new, suddenly popular browser makes an entry into this list, sometime in the future. Which is probably going to happen sooner than you think.

Please Upgrade Your Browser

One ironic way that browser detection bit developers in the past was a rampant practice in the early 2000s. Some of those sites are still around, so they can serve as a snarky reminder to focus on features and not browsers. Because Internet Explorer was so dominant and Netscape 4.*, the only other browser with any market share at all, was so horrible, it was common for people to sniff for Internet Explorer and leave an upgrade message for people running basically anything else. You will still see these warnings on some pages, except these days they are telling you to upgrade the latest Chrome or Firefox to Internet Explorer 6.

The Open Web Platform

Although the Web has always been a wonderfully messy and vibrant place, where sites can go from a sketch on the back of a napkin to a headline-making enterprise with a billion-dollar valuation in the course of a few months, the World Wide Web Consortium (W3C), the organization responsible for the standards that the Web is built upon, often moves more like it's overseeing transatlantic shipping in the 1800s.

If, in the early 2000s, you were the kind of person who paid attention to their activities, you could wait for *years* for anything interesting to happen. There was lots of discussion, lots of tweaking of existing specifications, and really not much else. Couple this with Microsoft shuttering Internet Explorer for lack of competition and slow (occasionally contentious) movement at ECMA, the organization responsible for the ECMAScript (the language commonly known as *JavaScript*) specification, and you can see how things stagnated.

Let's look at some dates to give you a sense of just how bad it was:

- In December 1997, the W3C published the HTML4.0 specification.
- In early 1998, they published the XML 1.0 Standard.
- In May 1998, the Cascading Style Sheets (CSS) level 2 specification was published.
- The ECMASCript Specification version 3.0 was released in December 1999.
- XHTML 1.0, the specification that redefined HTML as a subset of XML was published as a recommendation in January 2000.
- Internet Explorer 6 was released on August 27, 2001.
- SVG 1.0 became a W3C Recommendation on September 4, 2001.

After that, not much happened.

"Things" happened, of course. Meetings were held, road maps were prepared, and progress, of a sort, toward the Web of the future was visible in incremental revisions to standards. This orderly progress, to someone with only a passing interest in these sorts of things, probably seemed like a positive trend.

I sometimes felt like I knew *everything* about web specifications at the time, although I didn't really. Instead of spending time learning about new things on the horizon, *as there weren't any*, I used to do deeper dives into the existing specifications. I actually had binders with printouts of the xHTML1.0, HTML4.0, and CSS2 specifications. I could do that because things moved so slowly, those printouts stayed valid for a really long time.

The reality on the Open Web was different than any perception of "orderly progress." Out in the real world, the Web was busy taking over. Fueled by a heady mixture of popular interest, maniacal hype, gobs of money, and (for many people) an honest belief in the Web as a platform with the power to change the world, the Web was very quickly being pushed and pulled in directions the standards bodies never dreamed of when they were drafting their documentation. Compare the needs of the Web of the mid-1990s, when these standards documents were being written, to the Web of the dot-com era, and you'll see why so many problems fell to the creativity of web developers to solve. People had to be clever to bolt together solutions with the existing, somewhat limited, set of tools that were available.

Still, all the cleverness in the world wasn't enough to get around the main limitations of the standards and the browsers themselves. Something as simple as generating rounded corners for an HTML element was a topic worthy of dozens of articles, blog posts, and probably a patent or two.

Other topics were either practically impossible or took many years to solve. The many creative, technically complicated solutions to serving custom fonts over the Web fell into this category. Leveraging third-party technologies like Flash, Vector Markup Language (VML), and eventually Canvas, libraries like cufón and SIFR brought custom type to the Web through heroic individual effort and at the cost of third-party dependencies (and questionable licensing legality). This meant that even developers who believed in the Open Web Stack had to rely on closed technologies to simply get a corporate typeface onto the Web in a maintainable way.

Something had to give.

Web standards, Flash, and the rebirth of the Open Web Platform

All that really needs to be said about the immediate effectiveness of the late 1990s standards work is that the era that directly followed it was dominated by Adobe Flash as the platform of choice for anything even remotely interesting on the Web. Everything from financial dashboards and video delivery to the slickest marketing work was handled by Adobe's ubiquitous Flash plug-in. Unfortunately for people who believed that the Web was most effective when it was built on top of open standards, Flash provided a far richer platform for developing serious interactive applications and "cool" effects for marketing sites.

It became the de facto standard for deep interaction on the Web.

The core web technologies were basically ignored. The overall perception was that JavaScript was a toy language used for occasional form validation, CSS was poorly understood and even more poorly implemented in web browsers, and HTML was most useful as a dumb container for serving Flash files.

Throughout this dark period, there were still people championing these technologies and to a very large extent it's down to them that we're where we are today. From organizations like the Web Standards Project (WaSP) and the wildly influential mailing list/online magazine A List Apart, and through the work of individuals like Peter Paul Koch and Eric Meyer, the fundamental technologies that drove the Web were being reevaluated, documented, and experimented with at a furious pace. Quietly, invaluable work was being done documenting browser behavior, crafting best practices, and solving implementation issues. Although it wasn't the most fashionable work, there was plenty of activity using open standards in creative ways. That research and code served as the foundation for the revolution that would follow and change the course of the Web.

That revolution had two main drivers. One took place under the eye of the W3C itself, and the other came straight from the front lines.

The first event was the formation of the Web Hypertext Application Technology Working Group (WHATWG). The second was the astounding adoption of Ajax-based web development.

The WHATWG

The WHATWG was born at the W3C Workshop on Web Applications and Compound Documents in June 2004. This W3C meeting was organized around the new (at the time) W3C activity in the web application space and included representatives from all the major browser vendors, as well as other interested parties. There, in the first 10-minute presentation of session 3 on the opening day of the two-day event, representatives from Mozilla and Opera presented a joint paper describing their vision for the future of web application standards. This position paper was authored in response to the slow general pace of innovation at the W3C and the W3C's focus on XML-based technologies like xHTML over HTML. It presented a set of seven guiding design principles for web application technologies. Because these principles have been followed so closely and have driven so much of what's gone into the specifications over the last several years, they're repeated in full here. Some were driven by the mistakes of xHTML ("Users should not be exposed to authoring errors"), and others were driven by good sense ("practical use" and the desire for an "open process"). All have been visible in the process in the intervening years. The specifications are as follows:

Backwards compatibility, clear migration path

Web application technologies should be based on technologies authors are familiar with, including HTML, CSS, DOM, and Java-Script.

Basic Web application features should be implementable using behaviors, scripting, and style sheets in IE6 today so that authors have a clear migration path. Any solution that cannot be used with the current high-market-share user agent without the need for binary plug-ins is highly unlikely to be successful.

Well-defined error handling

Error handling in Web applications must be defined to a level of detail where User Agents do not have to invent their own error handling mechanisms or reverse engineer other User Agents'.

Users should not be exposed to authoring errors

Specifications must specify exact error recovery behaviour for each possible error scenario. Error handling should for the most part be defined in terms of graceful error recovery (as in CSS), rather than obvious and catastrophic failure (as in XML).

Practical use

Every feature that goes into the Web Applications specifications must be justified by a practical use case. The reverse is not necessarily true: every use case does not necessarily warrant a new feature.

Use cases should preferably be based on real sites where the authors previously used a poor solution to work around the limitation.

Scripting is here to stay

But should be avoided where more convenient declarative markup can be used.

Scripting should be device and presentation neutral unless scoped in a device-specific way (e.g. unless included in XBL).

Device-specific profiling should be avoided

Authors should be able to depend on the same features being implemented in desktop and mobile versions of the same UA.

Open process

The Web has benefited from being developed in an open environment. Web Applications will be core to the web, and its development should also take place in the open. Mailing lists, archives and draft specifications should continuously be visible to the public.

The paper was voted down with 11 members voting against it and 8 voting for it.

Thankfully, rather than packing up their tent and going home, accepting the decision, they decided to strike out on their own. They bought a domain, opened up a mailing list, and started work on a series of specifications. They started with three:

Web Forms 2.0
> An incremental improvement of HTML4.01's forms.

Web Apps 1.0
> Features for application development in HTML.

Web Controls 1.0
> A specification describing mechanisms for creating new interactive widgets.

Web Controls has since gone dormant, but the other two, Web Forms and Web Apps, eventually formed the foundation of the new HTML5 specification.

Score one for going it alone.

As was mentioned, they've stuck to their principles over the years. Arguably, the most important of these principles is the very open nature of the standards process in the hands of the WHATWG. Before the birth of the WHATWG, the standards process and surrounding discussion took place in a series of very exclusive mailing lists, requiring both W3C membership (which costs thousands or tens of thousands of dollars, depending on the size and type of your organization) and then specific inclusion in the particular Working Group under discussion. There were public discussion mailing lists, but those were far from where the real action was taking place. It was a very small group of people, operating in a vacuum, completely separated from the people working on these pivotal technologies on a day-to-day basis.

Instead of that exclusionary approach, the WHATWG made sure its activities were taking place in the open. If you subscribed to the mailing list and commented, you were suddenly part of the solution. This has led to vibrant, high-volume discussion feeding into the standards process. There are still many people involved who are far removed from the day-to-day business of making websites and applications, but there's also a constant stream of input from people who are knee deep in building some of the biggest sites on the planet.

It's not perfect, of course. They weren't kidding when they stated "every use case does not necessarily warrant a new feature." If you follow the WHATWG mailing list, it seems like not a month goes by without someone proposing a new feature, complete with valid use cases, and failing to get their proposal approved. This can end up being frustrating for all involved, and the mailing list has been known to get heated from time to time. For one example, months of discussion around a standardized mechanism to control the way scripts were loaded and executed went nowhere despite well-reasoned arguments from a number of high-profile sources. The discussion there has since restarted, so maybe this time it will stick. The lengthy, and oftentimes acrimonious, discussion of a solution for responsive images stretched out over a period of four years with a peaceful resolution only showing up recently, so there is hope.

Everyone isn't happy all the time, but the process works. Even with the hiccups and flame wars, things move much more quickly than they did at any period before the WHATWG was founded, and there's less confusion about how the decisions are made, even if people don't agree with them.

Ajax

On February 18, 2005, Jesse James Garrett, cofounder and president of design consultancy Adaptive Path, wrote an article entitled "Ajax: A New Approach to Web Applications." In it, he described a new, at the time, trend in apps like Gmail and Google Maps that focused on smooth application-like experiences. He coined the term *Ajax* to describe it and called the pattern "a fundamental shift in what's possible on the Web."

He was certainly right.

Garrett's post didn't invent the technology pattern, of course. It had actually been growing organically for several years, with the fundamental technologies in place as early as 2000. What the post did do was give focus to the trend with an intelligent, easy-to-understand definition and a very marketable name. With that focus, the pattern went from a vague collection of sites and apps tied together by a common design and interaction feel and technology stack, to being something that you could easily market and discuss. Instead of saying "I want to build a fast app that doesn't rely on multiple page loads like

Google Maps using standard web technologies," you could say "I want this app to use Ajax" and people would instantly get what that meant.

The immediate popularity of Ajax meant that a number of very intelligent developers started to take a look at the infrastructure for developing web applications in a cross-browser way. Before Ajax, standards-based development was mostly focused on markup and style, which was valuable when doing content sites, but didn't provide the full solution when approaching the complexities of a browser-based application. After Ajax, standards-based development included a dynamic, interactive component that drew engineers from other programming disciplines in droves. There were a lot of problems to solve, and it seemed like every company in America was looking for someone to solve them. Libraries like Prototype, Dojo, MooTools, and eventually jQuery rose up to fill in the gaps between the various browser implementations. These libraries, becoming more and more robust, eventually began to feed back into the standards process with common patterns being brought out of libraries and into the browser.

Tracking the Open Web Platform today

One of the great challenges of working on the Web today is keeping abreast of the changes in the standards space. This section will give you a quick guide to the current standards development landscape and will offer some hints on how to keep up to date with developments in the standards landscape.

The current standards development landscape generally breaks down as follows:

HTML and related APIs
> Main development of what's referred to as the "living standard" happens with the WHATWG (*http://www.whatwg.org/*). The mailing list archives (*http://www.whatwg.org/mailing-list*) are also online. This work is an ongoing extension of the work done for HTML5. A so-called "snapshot specification," HTML5 is currently a candidate recommendation at the W3C (*http://bit.ly/uw-html5*).

CSS
> CSS development has been broken down into smaller modules. CSS 2.0 was a monolithic specification that covered everything to do with CSS. For CSS3, the decision was made to break down the specification into specific features. This means there are some modules further along in the development process than others.

The W3C's big list of modules is available here (*http://bit.ly/uw-w3c-modules*).

ECMAScript
The ECMAScript mailing list (*http://bit.ly/uw-ecmascript*) is where all the action happens.

With the parallel tracks of the WHATWG kick-starting the standards process and Ajax making the intersection of HTML, CSS, and Java-Script some of the most important technical real estate in the world, the standards space went into overdrive and browser vendors started tripping over themselves to implement those newly minted standards.

On the surface, this is great—we get new toys!

There are a couple of downsides. One is that it's basically impossible to keep track of everything. For my part, I actively follow the development of the ECMAScript specification and the work of the WHATWG. That means I have to rely on other people to point out the cool work being done in CSS. And, even ignoring CSS, it's pretty easy to miss a couple of weeks or even a month or two of discussion on the mailing lists. You go away for vacation, and the whole thing might be turned upside down by the time you get back.

Another downside is that people, in the rush to implement new features in the browser or to experiment with them on the Web, sometimes make mistakes. Whether it's a poorly vetted specification; the well-meaning, but awkward decision to prefix experimental CSS features; the tendency of "new" HTML5 features to occasionally go away (like the loss of the hgroup element or the disappearance and subsequent reappearance of the time element); or the decision to implement an alpha feature in a site meant for human consumption, only to see it break in a later version of the target browser; the rush for the new and shiny has had its share of casualties over the past few years.

Navigating this space is important, though. As you'll see in one example in the section on responsive images in Chapter 6, following the standards discussion, learning about potential JavaScript solutions, and implementing standard stable patterns can produce great long-term benefit for your site. It's just sometimes tough to figure out when something is really *stable*, so the closer you can get to the discussions, the better. Not many people have the time needed to be involved in even a single feature discussion as an active participant, forget about the mailing list as a whole, but you really should have time to at least monitor the subject lines, checking in where applicable.

The ECMAScript specification is also being worked out in public. If I only had time to detail all the ins and outs of the ECMAScript-shaped black hole you can see on the standards timeline between the third edition in December 1999 and the release of the fifth edition 10 years later. The fact that they completely skipped over the fourth edition because it ended up being too contentious a process is probably all you really need to know. The good news is, the TC39 committee has patched up its differences, invited a bunch of workaday developers into the standards body, and generally been pretty great for the past few years. They're hard at work finalizing the sixth edition (aka ES6), which promises to be a revolutionary step forward in the development of the language. Work on ES7 and ES8 is also underway. Work on the ES6 specification also happens on a high volume, public mailing list and because of the way that the body is structured it's much easier for them to invite individual experts onto the committee.

Keep Your Résumé Handy

If you work somewhere that doesn't allow you even enough time to monitor the subject lines on these mailing lists and you're still relied upon to stay, to quote many a job description, "up to date with the latest technologies," then it might be time to have a talk with your boss. If there was any time to stay ahead of the curve, it's right now.

Connection Speeds and Quality

I've been interested in web performance since the 1990s. We didn't really have a name for it back then. I just remember reading that the optimal speed of a human–computer interaction is less than 100ms and thinking "on the Web, we can't do *anything* that fast." Download speeds alone were bad enough that 100ms was a tough task for even the simplest sites.

Unfortunately, even though download speeds and hardware specs have greatly improved, because developers and designers have consistently pushed the envelope (*http://bit.ly/uw-webpage-growth*) and designed for higher-performance hardware and faster connections than is the current norm, we're still seeing some of the same issues we did back then. With the addition of sketchy mobile networks into the mix, the question of connection speeds and bandwidth is still a serious issue.

We've got a more nuanced look at what makes a fast site these days and have dozens of tools at our disposal to figure out what's right or wrong with our pages. That's great. But until we change the way we approach making web pages and design to the reality of our audience and not what we wish their reality to be, performance is never going to be what it should be.

For one example, the grand master of web performance, Steve Souders, did some research and found that over 60% (*http://bit.ly/uw-bytes-per-page*) of the bytes on the Web are in images and that image payloads are only getting larger (*http://bit.ly/uw-img-payloads*). It's not unheard of for a site to serve more than 10MB–20MB for a single page. There have been examples, like one notorious one from Oakley (*http://bit.ly/uw-oakley*), of up to 85MB. It was a rich, visually exciting site. It also took minutes to load even on a broadband connection. People are struggling with ways to cut down image sizes but still satisfy the "big image" trend visible across the Web. Google, being Google, has even proposed a new, lighter-weight image format known as *WEBP*.

And that question doesn't really factor in the complexities of people browsing the Web over mobile networks. The reported speeds for the major mobile carriers have grown steadily, but the quality of connection on mobile isn't nearly what you can expect from a wired connection or even that of a cafe WiFi. Complete dead spots, holes in 4G coverage, train tunnels, signal concentration (try to get a signal at a heavily attended conference), and who knows what else (solar flares?) all conspire to make your mobile connection flaky. Add to that the demands that connections make on your battery (an HTTP connection means the radio has to make a connection to the local cell tower, that spikes the power usage on the device (*http://bit.ly/uw-mobile-connection*)), other limitations of mobile connections, and the expectations of users with metered bandwidth, and it's clear that you should be designing with the idea of limiting bandwidth as a primary goal.

This is especially true if you have a global audience. The whole continent of Africa, home to more than one billion people, basically skipped over the desktop altogether and will only ever connect to the Internet using a mobile device on networks of unknown quality.

Balancing performance, battery life, and bandwidth usage is a juggling act that will be touched on throughout this book.

The Human–Computer Interface

The marriage of the mouse with the graphical user interface launched the personal computer revolution. Being able to manipulate files and perform other tasks with the click of a mouse opened up the power of computers to the point where they took over the world. A second revolution in human–computer interfaces took place with the rise of touchscreen-enabled smartphones and tablets. One of the biggest challenges facing web developers these days arises from the fact that both of these interface paradigms are active on the Web. Trying to sort out what events to support and which design enhancements for touchscreens to enable is a hard problem to solve.

Even before widespread adoption of smartphones and tablets with touchscreen displays, there was complexity involved in properly coding for various human–computer interfaces. In addition to the mouse, providing keyboard-based navigation hooks and shortcuts has been an important, if neglected, part of web development both for power users and as a vital accessibility feature. With the flood of touchscreen devices, the picture became even more complicated. Everything from the size of buttons to the use of hover effects had to be reevaluated.

People initially tried to solve this problem by separating the world into two binary states—touch-capable or nontouch-capable. Touch-capable devices would get big buttons and gesture events and nontouch-capable devices would get the old-school web experience.

The thing is, it's not really a binary choice. From Windows 8 laptops to Chromebooks and even things like the Samsung Galaxy Note with its hover-capable and fine-grained stylus, there are many devices that can have a mouse, or mouse-like implement, in the case of a pen or stylus, and be a touchscreen at the same time.

Personally, there are moments when I'm doing artwork on my Windows 8 laptop where I'll have the mouse/touchpad, can touch the screen, and will be drawing with an interactive pen on a drawing tablet. What kind of user am I?

Adding to this already complicated story is the fact that the common detection for touch capability only reports whether or not the browser supports touch events by testing for the `ontouchstart` in the `windows` object, not if the device is a touchscreen:

```
if( 'ontouchstart' in window ) {
    console.log( "touch events are present in the window
        object" );
}
```

So, even if you wanted to treat it as a binary, you can't reliably do so.

We can't forget about the future, either. It's coming whether you want it to or not. Devices with "floating touch" already exist, which means the hover event might be activated by a finger gradually approaching the surface of the screen on a device with no peripheral mouse or stylus.

And taking the third dimension even further, how common will purely gestural interfaces like the Microsoft Kinect be in the years to come?

Producing robust interfaces that work with a keyboard, mouse, finger, or with a hand waving through the air (like it just doesn't care) is one of the most important challenges you face as a web developer today.

Screen Resolution and Orientation

One of the legacies we've dealt with as we transitioned from the world of print to the world of the Web was the desire for designers to have pixel-level control over every aspect of their designs when ported to the Web. This was somewhat possible when we had a limited set of screen resolutions to deal with and people designed fixed-width designs. These days, it's significantly more complicated as more and more designs are based on flexible grids, and the number of display resolutions has grown out of control.

In the early 2000s, the biggest questions we had about screen resolutions were around the transition between 800px × 600px and 1024px × 768px. It seemed momentous at the time, but it took the community years to decide to make the switch *en masse*. These days? The stats for my blog, HTML + CSS + JavaScript (*http://htmlcssjavascript.com/*), list 125 separate screen resolutions, ranging from 234px × 280px to such massive displays as 3840px × 1080px and 2880px × 1800px. Nine separate display resolutions each represent more than 5% of the total visits. Long gone are the days where you would open up a Photoshop template with a couple of guidelines set up showing a 960-pixel grid and then fold in different browsers. These days, figuring out which resolutions to target or whether to target resolutions *at all* is just the first question you need to tackle before launching into a design and development effort. Figuring out whether or not to leverage responsive web design or other techniques to tackle multiple resolutions is also a key decision. It's not the last, however. It's down to the point where things like the question of doing any preliminary design is on the table for some applications. These days, some people rely instead on quick, iterative design and refinement to create the look and feel for a site. This won't work for something whose sole purpose is to be a thing of beauty, I imagine, but for a lot of sites, it's a wonderful option.

Once you've got that sorted out, you've then got the difference between landscape and portrait display to deal with. That state can change one or more times per browsing session.

Although I'm sure people are tempted to start plastering something like "best viewed in the latest Chrome at 1920 × 1080" on their sites in order to get the best possible resolution for their design, it's only going to get more difficult to predict "standard" screen resolutions going forward, so your designs potentially have to take into account a broad range of resolutions.

Pixel Density

With the release of Apple's Retina-branded displays and the screen quality arms race that followed, the quality of displays on smartphones, tablets, and laptops has undergone a remarkable transformation over the past few years. Where once the highest quality displays were solely the domain of high-end design shops looking for the highest fidelity for their print design work, now incredible quality displays are in millions of pockets and laptops around the world. The bad news is that not every display is created equal, so there's a bit of a learning curve when it comes to dealing with these displays gracefully when building visually striking sites and applications.

For a long time, displays had a pixel density of either 72 or 96dpi (dots per inch). For a long time, this was shorthand for web developers to spot designers who were used to working in print. You would get a file, clearly exported out of Quark XPress (or later, Adobe InDesign) that was just gigantic because it was set to some print resolution. The design would be for a 1024 × 768 monitor, and it would be a 4267 × 3200 or larger Photoshop document. The first thing you would do would be to shrink the resolution down and hope that the design dimensions fit onto the typical screens of the time.

Then, along came smartphones, and that shorthand went away in a hurry. In fact, both sides of the designer/developer divide have had to relearn the ins and outs of preparing files for the Web.

Why? If you're near a standard desktop monitor, stick your face as close to it as you would your phone, and (with some exceptions) you should be able to *see* the individual pixels. With your face right up there, images will look blocky, and most importantly, text will be hard to read as details designed into the typeface will be blurred out for lack of resolution. This is what your smartphone would look like if we didn't have higher-density displays. Driven by the need to create crisp text and images on small screens while simultaneously providing the largest possible screen real estate, device manufacturers have all improved their pixel density. This started with devices that came in around 150dpi, most famously the branded Retina display from Apple. Nowadays, 300+ dpi displays are common.

So, great, right? What's the problem? Let's quickly take a look at *reference pixels* and *device pixels* to illustrate why this new reality has added complexity to our lives.

Device pixels are the smallest units of display on the screen. They're defined by the physical characteristics of the screen, so they're the part of this equation that's set in stone (or glass.) The *reference pixel* is a practical measurement built on top of the physical system. It's defined to be roughly equivalent to the size of a 96dpi pixel at arm's length, roughly 0.26 mm. High-density displays can have more than one device pixel per 0.26mm, but they will render your page at an effective 96dpi. This is pretty much seamless as CSS borders, backgrounds, type, and the like can be clearly calculated and rendered to match the expected reference pixels. These displays can also take advantage of the higher density to render clearer text as fonts are built to scale and the extra detail that can go into those reference pixels makes text clearer and much closer to the resolution you would see on printed matter.

The one major exception to this flood of benefits is with bitmapped images. Print designers have long had an opposite shorthand to their own little DPI test. Instead of getting files too large for the Web, print designers are used to being sent files prepped for the Web to use in print campaigns. If you've ever done this, you'll know from their feedback that you can't scale bitmapped images *up*. If you need to print an image at 300dpi, all the information for the full resolution of the image needs to be there or else it will look like junk. No matter what TV shows like CSI might try to tell you, there's really no push button "zoom and enhance" that will make a blurry image clear as day.

So, on the Web now, if you need to show a 200px × 200px image on a high-density display, you need to provide more than 200px × 200px worth of data. If you don't, your images will look crummy. The following example illustrates the difference. Consider the following markup. It shows two images side by side. The images are 240 reference pixels square as defined by the height and width attribute on both images. The first image file was exported at 240 pixels square. The second is 668 pixels square. In the source, it's compressed down to 240 pixels with the height and width attributes:

```
<!DOCTYPE html>
<html>
  <head>
    <meta charset="utf-8">
  </head>
  <body>
    <h1>The Uncertain Web</h1>
    <h2>Chapter 01</h2>
    <img src="react-graffiti-96.jpg"
      width="240" height="240" />
    <img src="react-graffiti-267.jpg"
      width="240" height="240" />
  </body>
</html>
```

In the first screenshot, from a standard density monitor, the two images are rendered identically (Figure 1-4).

Figure 1-4. A screenshot from a standard density display

The second screenshot, taken on a 267dpi high-density display (the Samsung Galaxy Note 2), shows the differences in quality between the two images (Figure 1-5). The dimensions are the same, in reference pixels, but the higher number of device pixels in the Note 2 requires additional data to render clearly.

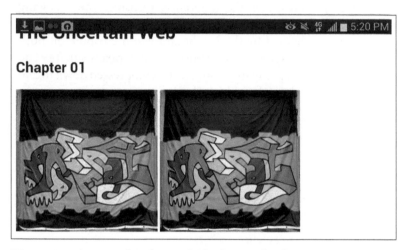

Figure 1-5. A screenshot from a high-density display

This is a thorny problem. As you've learned already, there are plenty of web users (billions) on crummy connections. Many web users are also on metered data plans and don't want to spend all their hard-earned money downloading data they'll never use. Serving those users the smallest possible payload with the best possible quality is key to creating great user experiences. On the opposite end of the spectrum, consumers with high-density displays ponied up the extra money for their fancy devices and want to get the high-end experience they've seen in the demos and TV commercials. They'll also notice that the negative fuzzy images stick out once you're used to the photographic crispness of a high-density display.

So, factoring in screen size, pixel density, and the size of the browser window itself means that there are suddenly a lot of factors to work through when dealing with bitmapped images. Do you serve everyone 2x images, scaling down for everyone, but in the end serving bytes that people on standard density displays aren't going to use? Or do you serve standard size images, sacrificing some blurriness for better performance in all browsers? Or do you bite the bullet and dive into the hornet's nest of responsive images? Add it up, and it's clear that trying to navigate the proper density of images is one of the trickiest areas of web development right now.

There are no easy answers on how to deal with it beyond using Scalable Vector Graphics (SVG) and forgoing bitmaps entirely (not always possible) or, drastically, not using images at all (even less possible in most environments.)

What's 2% Anyway?

If you've been thinking about these numbers and are already considering ways you'll cut corners, knocking browsers or screen resolutions off your testing and support matrix because they only represent 2% or 5% market share, it's worth taking a minute to think about what those numbers really mean. Based on your needs and requirements, you might be perfectly justified in many different support configurations. Although I strongly believe in supporting the largest possible percentage of web users, I also recognize that reality dictates certain support strategies. For example, working in financial services or health care, two industries that I've done a lot of work in, might require that I treat Internet Explorer 8 as a first-class browser. You, on the other hand, might be working on a site that caters to web developers and designers and might not see even 1% of your visits from IE8. So, instead of treating it as a first-class experience, you could provide simplified, alternative content or even devil-may-care support to IE8 users because *that's not your audience.*

It's useful to go examine your audience in this way whenever you're crafting support strategies. You might think you're comfortable with ignoring a certain browser from your testing plan, but then when you crunch the numbers and truly examine the makeup of your audience, you might realize that you'll probably need to spend some time testing in it or even craft some sort of optimized solution.

For one wildly unpopular example, according to Microsoft's IE6 Countdown site (*http://www.ie6countdown.com/*), IE6 still accounts for 4.2% of the global browser market. However that number stacks up against other stats we've seen, for the sake of argument, let's take their metric at face value. And anyway, Microsoft isn't looking to overstate the presence of a browser that, at this point, brings them nothing but negative publicity, so that's got to count for something. At first blush, 4% might seem like a small number, but that's before you really break down the numbers. For easy math, let's say there are

2,500,000,000 people out there with access to the Web. That puts that 4% market share at something like 100,000,000. For an easy comparison, that's just about the population of the Philippines, which just happens to be the 12th most populous country in the world. Looking at the numbers more closely, the high percentage of those Internet Explorer users in China (22% of the Chinese market) means that most of those users—80,000,000 or so—are Chinese. That puts the 100,000,000 IE6 users in a particularly Chinese context. That might mean you don't care because you have zero Chinese audience, but 100,000,000 users still means this is a choice you should make actively and not just with the wave of a hand because IE6 is annoying. If you're starting a site design and you're a global company, you have to ask yourself if you can safely ignore those users. Maybe you can, but it's safer to look at the question with as much information as you can muster instead of blocking your eyes and ears and assuming it'll all be OK. That way, when someone asks why you did or did not prepare for IE6, you can give a reasoned response.

Interestingly, desktop Safari also has around 4% market share. Most developers I know wouldn't dream of ignoring Safari, but at the end of the day it's still the same 100,000,000 people. Granted, it's *much* easier to develop for Safari, and the typical Mac user has enough disposable income that they can buy a Mac, so they're a more appealing demographic, but it does make for an interesting perspective.

For an even smaller slice, and one that has a different mind share (as it's mostly ignored instead of being hated), Opera Mini comes in at around 2% total market share by some measures. Most developers I've talked to have never tested with it and don't really know much about it. But its estimated 50,000,000 users are more than the population of California and Illinois combined. Would you ignore Chicago, San Francisco, and Los Angeles without a good reason? Probably not. Granted, Opera Mini has its own demographic quirks, but it shouldn't be completely ignored.

This isn't to say that you are somehow required to actively support any of these browsers. Not everyone has enough resources to design and develop for, test, and fix bugs across every device and browser. That said, it *is* important to keep some perspective and know what it really means when you're chewing over some of these numbers. At the end of the day, they may not matter to you, but you can't really make that decision unless you know what decision you're actually making.

Beyond your own existing analytics, there are several different resources you can look at to figure out the browser market:

- Peter Paul Koch writes intelligently about browser market share on this blog. (*http://bit.ly/uw-qb-market-share*)
- Stat Counter offers statistics based on billions of page views every month. (*http://statcounter.com/*)
- The Wikimedia Foundation publishes statistics based on the billions of page views generated by their own network of sites. (*http://bit.ly/uw-wikimedia*)
- Microsoft's IE6 Countdown clock is the best source of information about IE6's continued presence. (*http://bit.ly/uw-ie6-countdown*)

Also, with the number of cloud-based testing environments on the market and the fact that most design teams will have a variety of smartphones in the pockets of various members of the team, getting basic coverage isn't that hard if you decide to go for it.

This Is What We Wanted

Freaked out? Paranoid that the ground underneath you will shift at any moment? Good. Because it will. I'm not the type to predict things like space hotels and cryonic suspension in order to emigrate into the future (*http://bit.ly/uw-clarke*), but I can tell you there will be new devices, form factors, Open Web Platform features, and human–computer input modes that you'll have to deal with as a web developer for as long as the role exists. And really, this is the way it should be. The only reason everything was allowed to go dormant in the early 2000s was because competition in the space disappeared. Once true competition returned, the natural way of the Open Web, which is to be as crazy as I've just described it, returned with a vengeance.

The good news is, all of these devices, form factors, and browsers all share one thing. They work on top of the Open Web Platform: HTML, CSS and JavaScript. If you seize on this shared platform and try to create the best possible experience for the broadest possible range of devices, you'll be able to reach users in every nook and cranny of the globe.

The remainder of this book will look at ways to tap into the Open Web Platform in order to do that.

So let's look at how to make this happen.

CHAPTER 2

Navigating the Uncertain Web

> So I guess an escalator is stairs with progressive enhancement. Or those walkways in the airports that make you walk really fast. I guess that's just a floor that's been progressively enhanced. An electric toothbrush is a progressively enhanced toothbrush.
>
> — Jeremy Keith

So, now that you know what you're up against and are ready to wrap the whole Web in a big, inclusive bear hug, it's time to learn about some of the ways you can build widely compatible sites and applications.

What follows is a series of high-level ideas that will allow you to approach compatibility in a nimble way and piece together your own solutions to these issues when you're faced with the Web's uncertainty. If you're an experienced developer, then many of the lessons presented here might be familiar to you. Even if they are, looking at them in the context of uncertainty will likely give you new or different perspectives on the ways these concepts could be used to create compatible web solutions.

All of these concepts will be touched on and expanded throughout the book.

Read this chapter, get the conceptual flavor, and then you'll fill out the details with some of the technical samples in this book, with your own work, and with your own research. That said, it should be noted that some of these topics are worthy of a book of their own, so we won't be able to cover everything in detail.

Additionally, it will cement these concepts if, while reading this chapter, you start to apply these concepts to the kind of problems you face in your day-to-day job. If you're at an agency and building 2–25 projects a year, you're going to have different needs than a product person who might work on 2–3 releases of the same project every year, and you're going to seize on different aspects of this as important to you.

The one thing that I'll ask is that you read through this chapter with an open mind.

Don't Blame the Web for Being the Web

No, we didn't just diverge into the self-help section.

Hear me out, and I promise we'll get back to the technical pieces in just a second.

We've already defined that the Web is a diverse place that's getting more diverse every single day. That's pretty much impossible to ignore. So, if you accept the Web's diversity (and maybe even celebrate it), and you're getting angry about one thing (maybe Internet Explorer 8) or another (the stock Android Browser), just take a minute to remind yourself that *this is just the way the Web is.*

Repeat after me, *this is just the way the Web is.*

It's true. Unless we return to a new monoculture (sorry, Google, but I'm rooting against Chrome on that front), there's *always* going to be a "bad" browser. That's not magic, and it isn't a new concept. As soon as the current "bad" browser dies, the second-to-worst browser slots in to take its place. Google's Paul Irish wrote about it in 2011 with his post "Browser Market Pollution: IE(x) Is the New IE6 (*http://bit.ly/uw-bmp*)." Even ignoring Internet Explorer as an obvious bogeyman, if we'd had the WebKit monoculture some of you were hoping for a few years ago, we'd still have the frustrating gap between great browsers like Chrome and oddballs like the stock Android browser.

Getting yourself worked up about the Web having a spectrum of browser quality is like getting mad at the ocean for being wet. It's the price we pay for having access to anything that can connect to the Web.

The ability to deal with a varied environment gracefully is going to be one of your greatest strengths as a web developer. I've worked with, managed, and hired a lot of frontend engineers over the past 15 years. Without fail, the best ones were the ones that knew this intuitively.

I'm not insisting that you actively enjoy working with crummy browsers. I'm just like you. I want the most powerful tools available across the most possible browsers. I just understand that dealing with a wide variety of browsers is a core part of my job, so it doesn't drive me as crazy as it seems to drive other people. I can't guarantee it, but if you do the same, I think you'll be happier if you, too, accept the Web for what it is and get on with the business of making cool things.

Identify and Embrace Your Audience

You would think this would be automatic, but you'd be surprised how many times I've had to ask clients what browsers and operating systems their current users were using and what browsers and operating systems were important to them going forward. They often don't have this information at hand. The specific answers to these questions matter. You can look at web-scale statistics for browser and operating system market share to get some idea of where things are and where they're going, but the only metrics that truly matter are those for *your* audience. If you're redesigning Cult of Mac (*http://www.cultof mac.com/*), your browser and OS profile is going to be very different from the profile for the Microsoft Developer Network (*http://bit.ly/ uw-msdn*).

Different browsers reach a different percentage of users in different geographical regions. For example, if you're a global sports brand that outfits the heavy hitters of the sports world, with a large existing fan base in the People's Republic of China, it would be wise to notice the huge number of Internet Explorer 6 users in that country. Although it might not mean that you tailor your content for IE6 or limit what you do on newer browsers (there are lots of new computers, iPhones, iPads, and Android devices in China, too), it does mean there's going to be some attention paid to how the site operates when the browser's feature set is limited.

Why China?

It's come up a couple of times, so in case you're wondering, there are two basic causes for the persistent high percentage of Internet Explorer 6 usage in China: software piracy and software requirements at government and other large-scale sites. A great number of PCs in China are running pirated versions of Windows XP. Because people are wary of upgrading through Microsoft, lest their machines be somehow crippled by Microsoft, they're stuck running the default browser.

Perversely, because so many people are still running it and have historically run it, some government sites require IE6 in order to function.

For a few years now, Peter Paul Koch has been doing a series of deep dives into country-specific browser markets (*http://bit.ly/uw-qb-by-country*) on his blog. You should do some research with your own audience, but the insights he offers are an invaluable aid to the discussion.

As I can attest, having served as a consultant for some big banks and a fair share of health care companies, this same lesson about legacy IE applies to certain industries. Even in the United States, where older versions of IE are dying off, the numbers of pre-IE8 users in health care and finance are much higher than the rest of the Web as a whole. Like the users in China locked in by the regional administration requiring IE6, these users are often locked in because of the software requirements of legacy systems. Two of the largest companies I've worked with as a consultant were running Internet Explorer 7 as the only supported internal web browser until 2013. With both, I was focused on a broad range of browser support on my projects, so it wasn't like I was stuck in an IE7 time-warp, but it did factor into some of the decisions we made when building sites in those environments. I mean, if a site doesn't work on the CEO's computer, then it doesn't matter how well it plays in Chrome.

Obviously, knowing this kind of information in advance makes your life significantly easier. If, for example, you're planning on leveraging SVG for data visualizations, you would want to look at Raphaël (*http://raphaeljs.com/*), which has built-in support for legacy Internet Explorer versions rather than Snap.svg (*http://snapsvg.io/*), the successor which solely leverages modern browser features.

Or you may want to leverage progressive enhancement to create a bare-bones experience for legacy browsers of all stripes (Android prior to 2.3 doesn't support SVG either) and then layer interactive functionality on top of the basic experience.

Thanks, Dmitry

Both Snap.svg and Raphaël were authored by Adobe's Dmitry Baranovskiy. He's very much at the center of the SVG universe.

SVG came onto the scene in 2001 and was basically ignored by many in the web development world because of a lack of support in Internet Explorer and no clear API. Raphaël changed that by providing VML-based support for Internet Explorer and adding in a friendly, feature-rich API. Other libraries, like D3 (*http://d3js.org/*) and Highcharts (*http://www.high charts.com/*), have helped cement SVG's popularity, but Raphaël started the ball rolling.

So, if you're a fan of working with SVG (I am), thank Dmitry for opening up the floodgates.

On the flip side, if you look at your statistics and your site goals and you recognize that your audience is predominantly mobile, you will want to skip over some of the big images and heavy frameworks you'll find on desktop-centric designs and architectures. A lean, small-screen optimized design is going to serve the most important segment of your audience best, and if you do it right, you'll still be providing a fast, effective interface for your desktop users.

Of course, as the recent Slate redesign shows (Figure 2-1), you can go too far in embracing mobile and miss the mark for your desktop users. Many users echoed the sentiments expressed in Andrea Peterson's *Washington Post* article, "I Hate the New Slate. But It Wasn't Designed for Me. (*http://bit.ly/uw-new-slate*)" Their fully responsive design works very well on mobile devices. It's a solid, small-screen design that makes use of color, type, and selected photography to present a really great small-screen experience.

The desktop/large-screen view, on the other hand, feels like a slave to the small screen (Figure 2-2). Boxes fight for dominance, and their placement feels almost like chance. The single-serving cohesion of the small-screen experience becomes a large-screen experience without unity or hierarchy.

Figure 2-1. The Slate redesign seen in a small-screen configuration

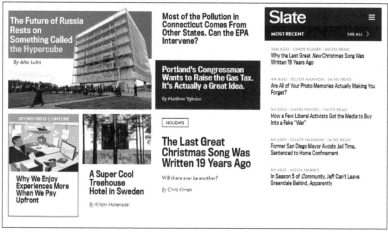

Figure 2-2. The Slate redesign seen in a desktop configuration

Test and Pray for the Best

Once you've identified your audience, where they are, and what they're using, it's time to define the technical demographics you're going to target. This will break down to the set of browsers, devices, and screen resolutions that make up your audience. Your job, once you've got some sense of whom you're targeting, is to figure out *how* to target them.

It's Never Too Late

Even if you're the caretaker of a project that's already out the door, these concepts can help you with your approach to both feature development and maintenance. It's better to have this information right off the bat, but if you don't, you can still use it, wherever you are in the software development lifecycle, to improve your site or application. Often, you'll hear "build for mobile first," but if your audience primarily uses desktop browsers, the opposite is just as valid.

Whatever you're doing, there are going to be types of users you'll really focus on. It might be everyone in the whole world on any web-connected device, or it might be mobile users from emerging markets. It'll probably be something in between. Regardless, you should have a pretty good idea of the capabilities and form factors your users will have. Once you have that, you'll want to come up with a testing and support strategy. This is the list of browsers and devices that you're going to test against and the profile of browsers and devices that you're going to support. At this point, no one is going to be able to test against every possible browser/device that they support. You can also break down the concept of support to include limited and full support.

Yahoo! Graded Browser Support

There was a time when all you needed to do was point your client or internal stakeholders to Yahoo!'s Graded Browser Support Matrix (*https://github.com/yui/yui3/wiki/YUI-Target-Environments*) in order to define a support strategy for your site. Yahoo! would assign every major browser a grade of A (primary development and QA support), C (baseline development and QA support, bugs fixed for catastrophic issues), and X (browsers that aren't developed against or tested against, but are expected to be capable browsers). Although the explosion of browsers and devices has rendered the support matrix itself less important, the concept of graded browsers still resonates in many corners.

For example, continuing with SVG as our key feature, imagine you're building a site to track workouts of runners. It will rely heavily on SVG in order to create interactive visualizations of the runner's pace, heart rate, and other metrics.

When you're working through these kind of questions, you'll want to leverage the site Can I Use… (*http://caniuse.com/*) heavily (Figure 2-3). Can I Use provides simple access to support matrices for a huge number of web platform features. Popping over to the SVG support page (*http://caniuse.com/svg*), you learn that native support for SVG is present in everything but older Internet Explorer versions and older Android devices.

As you can see with all the green numbers in Figure 2-3, that means you have a pretty wide range of supported browsers with full support for your key technology.

Internet Explorer 8 and Android pre-2.3 still represent a pretty large percentage of users, and you want to offer at least some level of support for them. You know Raphaël doesn't add SVG support to older Android devices because there's no VML there to hook into, so you may decide to add partial support to those browsers by creating static PNG representations of the visualizations on the server side and serving them as regular images.

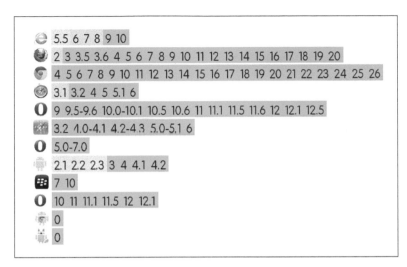

Figure 2-3. SVG support in early 2014 (data from caniuse.com)

With that general support matrix in place, the specific devices you'll test against really just depend on your time and resources. If you've got a big budget and a dedicated QA team, you might test against and require sign-off for more than 20 or 30 device/browser combinations. The following list is just a sample, but it gives you a taste of what a truly broad testing program would look like. This list also assumes you would test in multiple mobile browsers (Chrome, Opera Mini, UC Browser) on one or more of the devices.

This is a lot of work, but to really get this stuff right, you've got to do some hard work. That includes testing. The devices you should consider are as follows:

- Samsung Galaxy S3
- Samsung Galaxy S4
- Samsung Galaxy S5
- Samsung Galaxy Note II
- Samsung Galaxy Note III
- Nexus 5
- Kindle Fire
- Motorola Droid X (Android 2.3)
- Google Nexus 7

- Nokia Lumia 920
- iPhone 4S
- iPad 2G
- iPhone 5s
- iPhone 6
- Chrome (latest): Mac, PC, and a Chromebook
- Firefox (latest): Mac and PC
- Opera (latest): Mac and PC
- IE 8.0 on Windows XP
- IE 9.0 on Windows 7
- IE 10.0 Windows 7/8, including a touchscreen laptop
- IE 11.0 Windows 7/8/8.1, including a touchscreen laptop
- Safari 6.0

You're probably not going to have the resources or the buy-in organizationally to purchase and test on that many devices. Not many people can.

If that's the case, getting your hands on some dedicated testing devices (newer Android, something running Android 2.3, an iPhone, and an iPad) in addition to standard browser testing is the minimum you should do if you're truly serious about building compatible sites. If that sounds like you, your testing stack might look like the following:

- Samsung Galaxy S5
- iPhone 6
- iPad 2G
- Motorola Droid X
- Chrome (latest): Mac and PC
- Firefox (latest): Mac and PC
- Opera (latest): Mac and PC
- IE 8.0 on Windows XP
- IE 9.0 on Windows 7
- IE 10.0 Windows 7
- IE 11.0 Windows 8

- Safari 6.0

Unless you've got a lot of old hardware lying around, this assumes that you will use a virtual machine for at least some of the Internet Explorer testing.

This has a cost. Buying devices might run you $1,000–$1,500 or more, depending on your coverage. That might seem like a lot, but it's worth it. Do everything you can to afford some dedicated testing devices so that you don't have to resort to the phones in people's pockets as your "testing lab." That might sound like creative bootstrapping, but it doesn't work. People aren't going to be able to commandeer their coworkers' phones for several hours of intense testing. It's also a crapshoot whether or not you get coverage for the most popular devices.

In addition to whatever physical devices you have in your testing lab, you should look into augmenting your testing coverage with a cloud-based testing service. These services provide software-based virtual devices for you to test with. These services range from free to $10 or $100+ per month and can definitely enhance your testing coverage. However, these can't completely replace the benefit of testing a site in a real device in hand. You lose the ability to truly feel and experience the interactions, and you miss the way the site renders in the actual device pixels. As a secondary tool, however, these can be invaluable.

It's especially nice to be able to automate the taking of screenshots in a large number of browsers at one time in order to verify the rendering of the page through multiple iterations and form factors.

As a local alternative, both Apple and Google offer emulators (through Xcode and the Android SDK, respectively) for their mobile experiences. They're not as good as an actual device, but they often can do in a pinch. Chrome's Developer Tools emulation feature also works well. This feature allows you to crudely similute a "mobile" experience in Chrome. It's not an authentic experience, but it can be helpful to identify major issues.

China Once Again
Right now, the majority of the smartphone market in China is owned by local firms. China is also the largest smartphone market in the world. So, if you're concerned about China, you'll want to know about offerings from companies like Huawei (*http://www.huawei.com/en/*), Xiaomi (*http://www.xiao mi.com/en*), and Lenovo (*http://www.lenovo.com/*).

Yes, Lenovo makes smartphones. They're actually the third largest smartphone manufacturer in the world. (*http://bit.ly/ uw-lenovo-top*)

Whatever your scheme, the takeaway here is to become dedicated to testing as often as you can in as many browsers and devices as you can. People often perfect their site in one browser and then work backward from there, filling in holes in everything else. No browser is completely dominant anymore and the landscape is completely wide open, so getting as good an experience as possible in as many browsers as possible is the way to go.

The only way to do that is to truly experience the site on the targeted devices and browsers. Testing on a lot of real devices can uncover improvements that will improve your site in ways that you can't predict and will expose you to the experience your users are likely to see. This can both help to head off bugs and, more importantly, can feed back into the design process.

Focus on Optimal, Not Absolute Solutions

I'm a fan of single serving sites (*http://bit.ly/uw-single-serving*). Single serving sites are websites made up of a single page that do only one thing. Many are funny, some are clever (*http://isthisyourpaperonsin gleservingsites.com/*), and some are even useful (*http://www.downfor everyoneorjustme.com/*).

One, in particular, perfectly captures an issue I've run into plenty of times during the planning or design of a site. I can't tell you the number of times some question would come up about universal support for a design feature—for a blast from the past, think of rounded corners or the clean transparency of 32-bit PNGs. If the feature or design element was nonessential, my first instinct was always to push back for a simplified design in the offending browser. If there was strong resistance, even after explaining the development or performance cost of a workaround, I'd have to go into a well-practiced spiel about why it was OK to present slightly different visions of the site to different browsers. If I were smarter, I could have just thrown up Do Websites Need to Look Exactly the Same in Every Browser? (*http://dowebsitesneedtolookex actlythesameineverybrowser.com/*), and the answer would have been seen as clear as day (Figure 2-4).

Figure 2-4. A Screenshot from Do Websites Need to Look Exactly the Same in Every Browser?

Not that it would have made much of a difference. At one point, there was an idea, born out of print production I think, that the design of a site was an absolute thing. The look of a site in the PSD would be, *to the pixel*, the look of the site in every browser across every platform. As frontend developers, we were driven to extremes in order to achieve pixel perfection across browsers and operating systems, often having to explain things like the difference between scrollbars or form elements on the Mac and PC being something we couldn't really work around.

That site was actually written in reference to the differences between legacy IE and modern browsers. These days, although the difference between legacy IE and modern desktop browsers is still a concern, it's not the only place this idea manifests itself. When you bundle in the dozens of viable browsers and devices out there, there are so many places where the look of a site can diverge that it would be practically impossible to actually design an absolute look and feel for every possible permutation. An army of Photoshop production artists would be needed to craft all those pixels. Font rendering, pixel density, web platform feature support, screen resolution, screen aspect ratio, and a slew of other factors all aid in the divergences of sites from browser to browser and device to device.

So, as important as it was in 2008 to understand that adding rounded corners to a box in IE6 wasn't worth the effort, understanding that things will look differently across platforms, browsers, and devices is now a fundamental concept of web design and development. You will invariably have dozens of differences in the rendering of your site on different browsers and platforms.

And that's OK.

As part of that practiced spiel, I used to say that the only people who would look at a site in more than one browser were the people who were building it. Although that's not true anymore, as people will often visit one site on the desktop, on a tablet, and with a mobile browser, they're already used to differences between the different form factors. You're not going to shock them by showing them a different look on their phone.

It's actually a benefit—one that they'll hopefully notice. These days, the differences among browsers and platforms goes well beyond the surface. Each of those form factors might need distinctly different features or completely different designs to best satisfy the site's requirements in every form factor.

This idea needs to be part of your site's DNA. Your site is not an absolute thing. There is no one true vision of it. The best possible site you can have will be the best possible site for everyone that visits it. If that means it's a high-DPI, 25MB monstrosity for a guy on a Macbook Air in a coffee shop in Palo Alto, or just a logo and an unordered list for someone on a rented-by-the-minute feature phone in Lagos, then that's the way it is. Once you have this idea—that is, that you *can* and maybe *should* be presenting different views to different users—it's much easier to make intelligent choices based on the site's requirements and your audience.

The tough part of this is getting the message across to all the different stakeholders on a project. It's easier than it once was, because as I've mentioned, people are already used to seeing differences with different devices, but it's still something that you need to prepare people for from the start. This approach is most successful when it's called out early and often. The last thing you want is someone being confused by a static PNG in an old Android when everything else is getting a crazy D3 visualization. Instead, if you communicate your intent, they should expect it, understand it, and hopefully appreciate it for what it is.

Embrace Accessibility

Web accessibility ensures that people with disabilities can access the Web. In general, the goal with accessibility standards is to ensure that content is served and structured in such a way that users with disabilities can access it directly, or if direct access isn't possible because of their disability (audio content for a deaf user or a visual chart for a visually impaired user), to provide alternative content that conveys the same information.

Simply put, if your site is accessible, you're guaranteeing that you'll be able to reach the largest possible audience.

You're also doing the right thing. It's not all that difficult to create accessible sites, and the benefit for people with disabilities is enormous.

You should be doing this anyway, seriously.

Based on the 2010 U.S. census (*http://bit.ly/uw-2010-us-census*), 56 million Americans were classified as having a disability. That's 18.7% of the total population. Not all disabilities would hinder the ability of a user to access the Web, but by taking a deeper look at the data, we can start to see some numbers emerge. With the understanding that inviduals might have one or more class of disability, Table 2-1 shows the number of Americans with disabilities that might interfere with their use of the Web. Numbers for this are hard to come by, but even using these numbers as a rough guide, you can estimate that there are millions of Americans that rely on the accessibility of sites to use the Web.

Table 2-1. Disabilities that might interfere with use of the Web

Class of Disability	% of Americans	Total # of Americans	Note
Visual	3.3	8,077,000	
Hearing	3.1	7,572,000	
Motor	2.8	6,700,000	Based on the number of Americans with "difficulty grasping objects like a glass or pencil" as a rough analog for mouse use
Cognitive	6.3	15,155,000	Covers all mental disabilities

And that's just in the United States, where this data is readily available. Extrapolating these patterns to the rest of the world and those tens of millions of disabled users turns into hundreds of millions.

And, if doing the right thing isn't enough, as a bonus, creating accessible sites has the side effect of making your sites more usable by everyone and more compatible for all users.

Let's look at some specific examples. The following accessibility concepts, taken from the Web Content Accessibility Guidelines 2.0 Appendix B (*http://bit.ly/uw-accessibility*), will have a positive impact for *all users* of your site, especially users with small screens or low bandwidth.

Provide Text Alternatives for All Non-Text Content

If images fail to load or are loading slowly, alternative text can provide crucial context to users. Unfortunately, the behavior of this feature is cranky on mobile. This text is displayed almost universally on the desktop. The behavior of mobile browsers is varied. Figure 2-5 shows Firefox, iOS Safari, Chrome, Opera Mini, and Opera displaying a page with a broken image. Only two of the five display the alternative text. This is a defect that needs to be corrected. The original bug, with WebKit (*http://bit.ly/uw-wk-bug*), took eight years to fix (too late for the iPhone and stock Android browser in these screenshots). Hopefully, the related Blink issue (*http://bit.ly/uw-blink-issue*) will be fixed sooner rather than later (and fix Opera and Chrome).

Regardless of the current behavior, this is an issue that will be fixed in future versions of these mobile browsers, so it's worth adding the info even if it's not shown universally today.

Figure 2-5. What a broken image looks like in Firefox, iOS Safari, Chrome, Opera Mini, and Opera

Additionally, low bandwidth or bandwidth-metered users might have images turned off, which is an option that's available in mobile browsers like Opera Mini (see Figure 2-6).

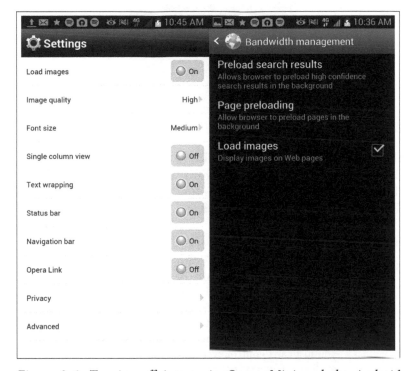

Figure 2-6. Turning off images in Opera Mini and the Android Browser

Providing alternative text fills in the blanks left by the ignored images (see Figure 2-7).

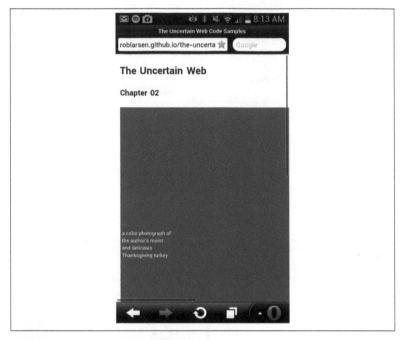

Figure 2-7. Opera Mini with images turned off

Alternative text is likely the accessibility you're most familiar with, but it's important enough to ensure that you're using them to proper effect. This checklist from the a11y Project (*http://bit.ly/uw-alt-text*) is a good place to start with improving your alt text.

 ### The Stock Android Browser Is Kind of Crazy
As Figure 2-7 shows, it's also very easy to manage bandwidth and turn off images in the stock Android browser. What is surprising is that with images turned off, the Android browser doesn't show alternative text *or* the contents of the title attribute. So let that serve as a reminder that any key information on a page should really be in plain text because you just can't control everything that happens in the browser. Even if you've got the most fault-tolerant CDN in the world, an Android browser user can just turn off your images, and they'll never see the important message you were trying to show them.

All of the recommendations around text alternatives to multimedia content also apply here. Text is cheap, bandwidth-wise, so it's a great added benefit (beyond the core accessibilty requirement) to offer text alternatives to video and audio content, such as transcripts, for low-bandwidth users or people who are simply in a rush.

Ensure Information and Structure Can Be Separated from Presentation

Good structure for your code makes it much easier to translate into different formats for devices with different capabilities and needs. This used to be a much bigger issue when people commonly used tables for layout, but it's still important now. You want your pages to make logical sense without styles and without JavaScript. If you can satisfy both of those requirements, you're in really good shape. One way to test how well you've structured your content is to view the document's outline (*http://bit.ly/uw-html5-outliner*) as defined by the HTML5 specification. If your document outline looks like a well-structured table of contents, then you're probably on the right track.

Make All Functionality Operable via a Keyboard Interface

Understanding the way that people without a mouse use the Web is an important (and neglected) exercise for everyone involved in making websites. You really should be testing everything you do without a mouse, and optimizing for keyboard navigation is one of the best things you can do for all of your users. This can manifest itself in a couple of ways. On the most basic level, making sure that common keyboard interactions behave in an effective, predictable way is very important. Tab order, skip links, and staying away from keyboard traps are all important to keyboard users. More advanced keyboard navigation is great for power users, as well as being a boon to users who can't use a mouse. My Gmail workflow is almost all keyboard driven. I crank through email like a demon. Many other big sites also have rich keyboard options built into their interface. Type "?" on any of your favorite sites to see if they, too, have keyboard shortcuts defined. Here's the overlay showing GitHub's rich selection of keyboard shortcuts (Figure 2-8).

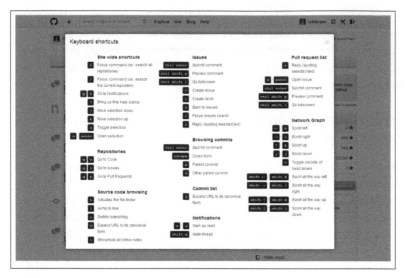

Figure 2-8. Keyboard shortcuts on GitHub.com

Satisfying this requirement also helps you think in beneficial ways about your site interaction model and the way that people can get to your content. If you avoid complex mouse movements and unclear interactive elements, you will make it much easier for users of all stripes to use your site. This includes those users on small screens and those using an imprecise "pointer" (their finger) to access your interface.

Content Can Be Paused by the User Unless the Timing or Movement Is Part of an Activity Where Timing or Movement Is Essential

The intent of this guideline is to ensure that visually impaired or cognitively disabled users have time to digest your content. This can manifest itself in different ways. The success guidelines (*http://bit.ly/ uw-success-gl*) talk about using turn-based games and having no time limit on online tests. Additionally, ensuring that video, audio, and time-based visualizations can be controlled by the user is an important component of this guideline.

A very common example I like to share is to avoid automatically refreshing content after a set period of time or to allow that functionality to be turned off. Think of a news site that refreshes every couple of minutes for the possibility of breaking news (and to inflate page views) or a sports site that refreshes a page automatically to show updated scores.

Simply put, don't force updates down your user's throat. In addition to the accessibilty concerns, all users can benefit from avoiding this practice. On mobile, for example, this rule is important for all users because battery life, bandwidth, and processor time are all significant factors in the overall mobile experience. You don't want to download unnecessary updates, wasting kilobytes of data and battery life.

Provide Mechanisms to Help Users Find Content, Orient Themselves Within It, and Navigate Through It

This is just good sense, of course, but is especially true when dealing with smaller screens. Make links make sense, give a good sense of where users are within your site or application, and give them multiple ways to reach content. The less you ask a mobile user to do to get to their important content, the better. I know the flashy demos of the latest iPhone or Galaxy phone make everything look like a magical trip through a land populated by magical tech fairies and black turtle-necked elves (all to a catchy college radio soundtrack), but it's hard to do things on a phone sometimes. Operating a phone with one hand, in the cold, while on the move, trying to get to an appointment on time? Yeah, that's exactly the time you want to have to sort through some random noise on a page looking for the "contact us" link.

For someone living that experience, *and we've all lived it*, having a clearly labeled "contact us" link with a big fat button that takes users to a simple list which includes your telephone number is worth more for the customer's experience than pretty much anything else you can do on the Web. You might have the most beautiful site in the world, but if your customer can't find your phone number, you might as well have made your site out of sticks and glue. It's useless.

USA.gov (*http://usa.gov/*) handles this without any fuss, providing a clearly labeled tel protocol link at the very top of its homepage in responsive mode. There's no mystery here how to get in touch with them, and the telephone link is available without a second click (Figure 2-9).

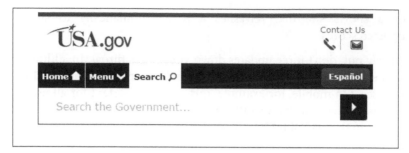

Figure 2-9. An easy-to-use phone link on USA.gov

Help Users Avoid Mistakes and Make It Easy to Correct Mistakes

It's hard to fill out forms on the Web. The more help you can give users, the better. This is true for all users.

What's interesting is that the work that's become the HTML5 specification actually started life as work on forms, and a large segment of the new specification is built upon new form inputs, APIs, elements, and attributes. You wouldn't know it looking at the demos and articles written about the Open Web Platform or in the slow support for these new features, even in the best browsers. Forms are generally neglected as a drudgery, even by browser vendors. Adding a new input for telephone numbers isn't nearly as sexy as adding WebGL and coding a JavaScript port of Quake. The thing is, people make money on the Web with forms—filling them out for a status update or tweet or to buy a book on Amazon.

The more time and care you spend on your forms, the better off you'll be. Making it difficult for people to make errors, offering meaningful error messages, and designing forms to lessen the user's cognitive load are going to directly affect your bottom line.

For example, offering inline validation (checking the form data for validity as a user enters it) and providing help text in context can help users more confidently enter the correct information in form fields. The Microsoft account sign-up form shown in Figure 2-10 illustrates both of these in action.

Figure 2-10. Creating a Microsoft account with inline validation and contextual help

Support Compatibility with Current and Future User Agents (Including Assistive Technologies)

I hope you recognize this concept at this point. This is, basically, the point of the book. I want you to produce sites that will work on everything that understands HTML now and in the future.

The fact that the first website ever made (*http://bit.ly/uw-first*) still works is a guiding principle here. Don't back yourself into a corner, and you'll be sitting pretty in 2025.

I will say that getting a basic understanding of how assistive technologies work and how they may work in the future is a good idea to add onto the understanding of the browser and device market. You *can* implement these rules without testing. The Web is full of active guidelines and conformance checkers for building accessible sites, but it makes a big difference when you really understand how these markup and code patterns actually interact with assistive technologies.

Don't Stop There

All the WCAG guidelines are going to make your site more robust for all users. The previous examples were just a few cherry-picked ones that were obviously tied into some of the principles we're exploring here and had obvious benefit for all users.

Also, in addition to these existing rules, it's important to assess the compatibility and accessibility impact of new technologies and technology patterns. Issues like the 300ms delay for tap/click on touch devices (*http://bit.ly/uw-click-delay*) (to disable or not disable) and the use of icon fonts (*http://bit.ly/uw-icon-fonts*), which may or may not load in older browsers, are multifaceted problems. You need to actively assess these issues as they surface, or you could end up with an accessibility nightmare that bleeds across to all your users.

Lose Your Technology Biases

Tech folks generally have great hardware and new, high-powered smartphones and tablets. Most other people in the world don't. Tech folks tend to forget that.

I know what you're thinking. Your company is super cheap. They haven't bought you a new laptop in two years. You don't even have a solid-state disk drive.

Oh, the humanity.

Cheap is a relative measure. On the hardware side, even with companies that are "cheap" with developer hardware, where the computers might be two or even three years old, you're not doing so poorly. Those machines were high powered when they were new. They have a ton of RAM and have had a corporate IT department whacking them into shape with updates and maintenance. You probably have two huge monitors and are on a monstrous network. The average consumers are going to buy the cheapest machines they can find, and then they'll run them into the ground. There are certainly exceptions to this— gamers come to mind—but for the most part, assuming great hardware is a mistake.

On the smartphone side, although there are certainly people across all walks of life who upgrade their smartphones for full price, outside of their contract (those lines outside the Apple store aren't there because everyone's contract is up), there are a lot more gadget-obsessed people in the technology space. I can't even keep track of what phone some of my friends have from month to month.

Technology people are also much more likely to own Macs than the average consumer. Just 5% or 6% of the global desktop market is Apple, but look around at the average tech conference, and it's often a sea of Macs. People are easily blinded to the reality that Macs remain a small minority on the desktop.

Developer (derisively): "Who uses Windows anymore?"

Me (sighing with an ache that would shake the cosmos): "More than a billion people. That's all. No need to worry about them, obviously. Go back to optimizing the site for Safari on a brand new Macbook Air."

None of these setups are anywhere close to the experience of the average user. Thinking that the typical developer and designer experience is at all "typical" and developing toward it is a longstanding problem, one made much worse by the broad variation of devices, operating systems, and browsers in the current ecosystem.

There are many examples of where this can be a real problem.

The iPhone Is the Only Mobile Experience

At the height of the iPhone's dominance as a mobile platform, it was typical to base mobile web designs on the interface and interaction model of the iPhone.

I wasn't a fan of that approach to begin with, as I think the Web should embrace the Web, and not copy some other platform, especially one that's trying to *strangle* the Web.

It became an even worse idea as the iPhone rapidly ceded the title of the dominant mobile platform to Google's Android. Nowadays, with Android up over an eye-watering 80% and iOS treading water, iPhone-style web interfaces are obvious byproducts of a bygone era.

Let me share one specific example of why this was a problem beyond the overall awkwardness of serving iOS-style designs to people who are on some other OS. Knowing the design tribe's deserved allegiance to Apple, I'm sure the following has happened more than the few times I've seen it.

As you probably know, iOS applications insert a back button into the application UI. There's only one button on the iPhone, so you need a software back button to navigate. In a world where the iPhone is the only game in town, inserting a back button into your web UI is therefore a good idea. The thing is, the world is pretty blanketed in Android phones right now, and every Android device has a back button built in, either as a dedicated software button on the screen or as a physical button on the device. All of them. It's required, and it also gets used *all the time*, so a back button in the UI of a web app, for an Android user, is a foreign experience. You're just wasting precious pixels. But yet, people do it because the iOS experience is all they know.

Closed. Won't Fix. Can't Reproduce.

"That animation is super fast on my machine."

Another painful example of the trap that tech folks fall into is with JavaScript performance.

Although there's a lot of talk about being "jank free" (*http://jank free.org/*) and the web performance community has grown to be a real force in the industry, the plain fact is most people don't look critically at their application performance in enough devices to truly get a sense of how it runs. As we've discussed, there are underpowered mobile devices, old desktops, and old browsers aplenty out there waiting to expose problems with your site. And really, with some of these setups, it's not just a question of poor performance. You can easily trip long-running script errors (*http://bit.ly/uw-long-running*), freeze the screen, and even crash the browser if you're not careful. If you think you're getting a second look from a user whose browser you just crashed, you've got another thing coming.

Now, obviously, there are simple code-optimization issues you can run into when working in JavaScript that can cause problems no matter what your setup is. Even in the latest Chrome, you can do things in one pattern that might be 10, 20, or even 100 times slower (*http://bit.ly/uw-for-loop*) than a different pattern that produces the same output. It's just that any of the latest generation browsers are so fast that, coupled with good hardware, they're going to mask problems that older browsers or crummy hardware will choke on. It's said so often that it's a cliche, but the reality is that it can "work on my machine" only to fail on some other hardware/browser combination.

Contrary to Popular Opinion, Internet Explorer Does Exist

This has driven me nuts for more than 10 years (see Figure 2-11). People don't test enough in Internet Explorer.

Figure 2-11. More than 10 years of Internet Explorer logos

Trust me on this. Whether it's Windows-based developers working all day in Firefox or Chrome or developers on a Mac not wanting to fire up Parallels, people don't test in IE early or often enough.

That's crazy.

I know it's the bogeyman, but it remains a huge portion of the browser market. Depending on where you look for your stats, it's got a larger market share than Firefox and Safari combined. Yet, people treat it like an afterthought. This is less of a problem than it was six or seven years ago because IE's market share has halved, but it's still a major issue when you're ignoring hundreds of millions of potential customers.

I've managed a lot of developers and projects over the years, and I've had specific feedback on this issue from folks who worked for me on several different occasions. This is especially problematic, as I've done a lot of consulting and agency work for health-care companies, financial services firms, and law firms. There's a *lot* of Internet Explorer in those industries. As I mentioned previously, it's often the *only* browser allowed on internal networks.

From a personal perspective, the single worst day of my life as a consultant was because of this phenomenon. One day, I returned to my hotel (in the absolute middle of nowhere), after doing an all-day workshop, ready to get dinner and then do my best to forget that I was trapped in the middle of nowhere with nothing to do but cruise around in my rented Toyota Yaris. Instead of that, I was blessed to discover that another project I was managing had broken in Internet Explorer before an important sprint deadline because a developer (Mac-based) had checked in code (it turned out) with a trailing comma in a Java-Script object. That particular catastrophic error indicated that he hadn't even opened the site in Internet Explorer (the target browser for the organization we were working with) before checking his code. If he had, he would have seen the site fail catastrophically.

And then he went away for the weekend.

Which meant I got to debug his code remotely, from a hotel room in the absolute middle of nowhere.

Some people would blame IE for my crummy night, because it's the bogeyman. Two things about that thought. First, IE can't win. They lose when they don't follow the specification, and they lose when they do. It's true. The ES3 specification didn't allow trailing commas in object literals. Crazy that the IE implementation could be to the specification. Secondly, the developer is to blame because he didn't test his code and checked it in. Blaming IE for that is like blaming the rain for getting you wet if you walk outside without an umbrella.

I think this behavior is at least part of the reason why people have such a visceral dislike of IE, including later versions, which are actually quite easy work with. Because so many people save IE for later in the development process, or downright ignore it, their only experience with the browser is one of shock and betrayal.

If IE were constantly sneaking up on me and punching me in the face because I wasn't paying attention, I'd be mad at it, too.

I've actually started to see this same response start to creep into developers who spend all day in Chrome when they decide to test in Firefox. It's not quite an epidemic yet, thankfully.

Embrace Empathy

Don't blind yourself to what your audience actually is by assuming that they are just like you. They're not. Your average experience at work, at home, or on your phone is almost certainly an optimal view of your site. Make sure you look at it, really look at it, in every scenario you can muster. Sure, we're all guilty of demoing code under the best possible circumstances. That's natural. The thing is, that demo is the ideal vision of your site. The thing you're actually building, the down-and-dirty version, is for people with a completely different relationship with technology than yours.

Try to get in their shoes instead of assuming everyone else is in yours.

You can accomplish this in a few ways. If your company does user testing or monitored usability sessions, sit in on them to see how your users actually interact with your site or application. This can be an incredible experience and is often only seen from the design or user experience side, so adding a development voice is a big deal for all involved and can help you get a sense for what your users are all about.

Lose Your Stack Biases

I've done a lot of work creating standard baseline (*http://html5boiler plate.com/*) tools (*http://bit.ly/uw-ant-build*) and documentation (*http://bit.ly/uw-code-standards*) for frontend development (*http://bp.sapient-lab.com/*), so you'd think I'd be the first person to argue for setting up an optimal stack and sticking to it.

I'm actually not.

Although I do think *limiting* the number of available tools is useful (because having everything available to everyone is just crazy), I don't think, in this day and age, proscribing a definitive frontend stack is useful.

I'm a proponent of using the right tool for the job, so the search for the "one stack to rule them all" seems like a waste of time to me. If you craft a perfect stack for creating single-page apps and then end up building a bunch of page-to-page content sites, you've wasted time and resources with a stack that's not suited for the work you're doing.

Now, if you're building a single monolithic product or site, you will obviously settle on one stack, because you've just got the one thing to build. But if you're working on multiple projects or sites in a given year, limiting yourself to the "one stack" is the wrong way to go.

Your users don't care if your stack is clever. They don't care how powerful your libraries are, how nifty your debugging tools are, or how easily you can just whip up a demo. What they care about is the speed, usability, look and feel, interactivity, and features. If your stack isn't adding to one of those, then you might be going down the road to stack obsession.

Certainly having tools you're comfortable with is important, but at the end of the day developer comfort isn't the most important part of this equation. The experience of the users of your site trumps everything else. Or at least it should. To that end, doing things like pushing 1 MB of fancy framework JavaScript down the pipe on a site that's meant to be consumed on a mobile device over a potentially dicey connection is simply a terrible idea. It doesn't matter how easy it makes your life if no one is actually going to use the site you're going to build.

This stack obsession manifests itself in many ways. Here are some of them and ways you might want to short-circuit the impulse and better serve your users.

jQuery

I'm a big fan of jQuery. Its fluent interface (*http://bit.ly/uw-fluent-interface*) is a joy to work with, and it's done more than any other codebase to popularize JavaScript. Still, one of the important reasons to use jQuery, beyond the interface, is to smooth over cross-browser differences in JavaScript implementations. These aren't solely related to legacy Internet Explorer (Dave Methvin actually says that "jQuery Core has more lines of fixes and patches for WebKit than any other browser" (*http://bit.ly/uw-methvin*)); however, a lot of the main differences are, so depending on your target audience and the skill level of your team, you might be able to skip it. Although jQuery started off as a lightweight alternative to beasts like Prototype, it's still around 30 KB gzipped and minified. In order to save those bytes, it's an option to write raw JavaScript or potentially leverage a smaller, jQuery-like library like Zepto.js (*http://zeptojs.com/*) (10 KB) instead. It might seem like a small gain, but if you're in the mindset of trying to save every possible byte, it is an option.

Personally, I stick with it because I like using it and worry about saving bytes in other places. The 30 KB will only be a noticeable download over the very worst connections (2 GB or crowded WiFi), so it's not a place where I would look to optimize.

 Use with Caution
Rick Waldron (TC39/Bocoup), Boris Zbarsky (Firefox), John-David Dalton (Microsoft), and Paul Irish (Chrome) actually put together a list of all the browser bugs the jQuery 2.* branch fixes (*http://bit.ly/uw-jquery2-branch*).

MVWhatever

One of the hottest areas of innovation on the frontend over the past few years has been the creation of frontend model-view-controller (MVC) style libraries and frameworks. Although many of them quibble about the acronym (MVVM, MVP), they all bring a common backend pattern to the frontend and enable a new approach to frontend application development. Angular (*http://angularjs.org/*), Backbone (*http://backbonejs.org/*), and Ember (*http://emberjs.com/*) are all popular entries in this space. They are powerful alternatives to the DOM-centric approach of libraries like jQuery and the general DOM-based application development we've been practicing for many years. Personally, I've spent the last couple of years working with Angular regularly, and I love it. It's fun, incredibly powerful, and has a strong, Google-backed community surrounding it.

The thing is, these libraries and frameworks are really designed for application development, so although they are super powerful tools, they shouldn't be grabbed for in every circumstance.

For example, using one of these libraries in place of tried-and-true server-side templating for a content site doesn't make sense. It's very much the same sort of pattern (variables from some data source are plugged into some sort of text-based templating engine), but there are no real benefits to doing it on the frontend.

When we first started learning about web performance, one of the fundamental lessons was that most of the performance hits on the page happened in the browser, not on the server. Templating on the server wasn't a performance problem for most people.

Why, then, are we rushing headlong to push functionality that was handled perfectly well by the server down to the frontend? Why, when the goal is to simplify and lighten the payload in the frontend, are we willingly passing a task that was solved 15 years ago on the server to the browser? Having to download a framework, as well as any other dependencies, is going to slow your site down. Downloading Ajax requests with the content data, parsing it, and inserting it into the DOM is also a performance penalty. We've learned to minimize the number of DOM traversals and manipulations. Why add more when the server can send a rendered page on the back of one HTTP request? It doesn't make sense.

Also, if, for some reason one of the JavaScript resources doesn't load, someone visits with an old browser, or someone visits with JavaScript turned off, you might end up with nothing but a blank page. That's just awful.

Use these powerful frameworks responsibly.

Keep at Least One Eye on the Cutting Edge

"HTML5" is the buzzword of all buzzwords, but the specification (*http://bit.ly/uw-html5*) you can go read is actually an older snapshot of what WHATWG editor Ian Hickson calls the "living standard." (*http://bit.ly/uw-hickson*) The work happening at the WHATWG is ongoing, important, and is often solving problems that are keeping us up at night, right now.

> **Polywho?**
>
> In case you were wondering, the term "polyfill" was coined by Remy Sharp. He describes his reasoning for the name in the blog post "What Is a polyfill?" (*http://bit.ly/uw-sharp*)
>
> Paul Irish provides a nice definition of a polyfill: "A shim that mimics a future API providing fallback functionality to older browsers."
>
> Alex Sexton coined the term "prollyfill" for "a polyfill for a not yet standardized API." (*http://bit.ly/uw-prolly-tweet*)
>
> Both of these terms and associated concepts are important ones when dealing with emerging APIs. If you follow the mailing lists, you will see the availability of potential polyfill options is often a factor in deciding whether or not an API is viable. Although it's not the only factor, there are many ES6 features that aren't possible to be polyfilled (although they can be handled with preprocessors like TypeScript).
>
> Polyfills will be discussed in more depth in Chapter 3.

We've already talked about the standards process a little bit. When it works, it goes a little something like this:

1. Someone comes along and proposes some feature along with a well-defined use case.

2. Everyone comes together—the standards people, reps from the browser vendors, and experts from the front line working through proposed solutions until a well-formed API surfaces.

3. The API will be published in a form that can be used as a blueprint for development.

4. Browser vendors will go off and implement solutions available in early release channels, like Chrome Canary or Firefox Aurora.

5. Developers who like living on the edge, including the wonderful folks working as developer advocates at the browser vendors, will work with the new feature giving feedback and honing the API.

6. Feedback will be assimilated and eventually the feature will be made available in the regular release channels free for all of us to use.

Of course, it's usually much messier than that. Web standards can be downright ugly at times. The multiyear, multiproposal, multicontroversy responsive images slow-motion trainwreck is a prime example of that. Four sometimes acrimonious years of proposals, setbacks, counterproposals, and flame wars have finally brought us a full suite of solutions to the responsive image use case, but the journey has been a tough one.

Still, no matter what sort of development you're doing, you'll have some pet problem that you're looking to tackle. Whether it's responsive images, or mechanisms to manage loading script files, or techniques for measuring web performance, there's going to be one potential feature that you're going to really care about. At worst, keeping tabs allows you to plan ahead and learn about the potential polyfill or prollyfill solutions as early as possible. At best, you can influence the process by taking part in the discussion, giving feedback on the API, doing early tests of the browser implementations, or writing a polyfill solution and sharing it with the community. The closer you can get to the latter scenario, the better, of course.

The good news is, if the new technology is one that has a reasonable polyfill path, you can start using the new API immediately and reap the benefits of native performance when the feature makes its way into web browsers. You've been future-proofed (unless the specification changes and that feature is removed).

We'll look at this in more detail when we look at images in Chapter 6, where we talk about the long, strange (frustrating!) march of responsive images through the standards process.

Spread Your Wings (and Question Your Assumptions)

Hopefully this chapter has already gotten you thinking about the way you've approached web development up until now. I'm assuming at least half of you think I'm an idiot. If so, I must be onto something. Whatever percentage of these concepts you agree with or feel are applicable to you and your particular situation, the biggest takeaway is the urge to question your assumptions. The things you hand-wave away *might* just be fine. Or they may be a problem causing some percentage of your users to have a crummy experience. You can't know the difference unless you take a second to really understand the issue.

Now that we've gotten the strategic approach to embracing uncertainty out of the way, it's time to start looking at practical ways to improve your odds of creating cool, compatible experiences.

The next chapter introduces feature detection, Modernizr, and polyfills, which will be used throughout the rest of the book. It's a small chapter, but is very important for the concept of feature detection, for the technical ins and outs of developing with Modernizr and using polyfills. The remaining chapters will examine individual problems, work through the issues with each, and then present a solution, or range of solutions, that you can use going forward.

Fun times ahead, I promise you.

CHAPTER 3

Lay a Foundation for the Future with Feature Detection and Polyfills

I am the last and highest court of appeal in detection.

— Sherlock Holmes, *The Sign of the Four*

One of the greatest challenges in developing modern websites is managing the broad range of device and browser capabilities present in the current ecosystem. One of the core ways to do this is via *feature detection*, testing for the presence of specific web platform features. This is compared to doing browser detection by looking for specific characteristics in the user agent string and coding for some specific version of Mobile Safari or Internet Explorer. That's the way people used to do things. There are still some use cases for doing browser detection (one is actually covered in the next chapter), but most of the time you want to think about feature detection, which is the concern of this chapter and is the more commonly recommended approach in modern web development.

Although you can roll your own solutions, the best option for feature detection on the modern Web is with an open source project called Modernizr (*http://modernizr.com*). Modernizr is a feature-detection library that makes it easy to test for dozens of web platform features, with a catalog of features growing by one or two a month. This chapter will look at feature detection in general, introduce Modernizr, show you how to download and customize the library, and illustrate three common patterns for leveraging Modernizr's feature detection in order to smoothly work around a range of browser capabilities.

If you're looking to do broadly available sites and applications, then mastering Modernizr is vital to your well-being.

This chapter will also look at the concept of polyfills and how they can help you experiment with bleeding-edge features in a future safe way. Additionally, you'll learn about common features that need testing and how to handle common support scenarios using polyfills or other fallbacks. *Elementary* (Figure 3-1).

Figure 3-1. Sherlock Holmes, illustration for "The Adventure of the Cardboard Box" (Sidney Paget, 1893; courtesy of Toronto Public Library (http://bit.ly/uw-sherlock))

Feature Detection

Let's start with a look at the basic concepts behind feature detection and also look at how feature detections are written.

The core concept of feature detection is actually ancient in web years. We were the cool guys testing against `document.all` and `docu ment.layers`, the two different and competing methods of accessing DOM elements, back when DHTML was the hotness.

I speak of the 1990s.

Say you wanted to write a cross-browser implementation of the (at the time) fancy new DOM method, `document.getElementById`. You could do something like the following and test against the W3C method, the Internet Explorer method, `document.all`, or the abominable Netscape property lookup in the `document.layers` collection, and then return the proper element:

```
function byId(id) {
  if (document.getElementById) {
    return document.getElementById(id);
  }
  else if (document.all) {
    return document.all[id];
  }
  else if (document.layers) {
    return document.layers[id];
  }
}
```

The importance of feature detection has grown over the years. Back when the browser landscape was binary and an obsessive developer could basically keep the entire web platform in (human) memory, it was very useful. These days? With thousands of pages of specifications fragmented over the browser spectrum we examined in Chapter 2, detecting for web platform features is going to help stop you from going insane. With the Open Web Platform changing daily, and powerful new features coming online all the time, the ability to use the latest and greatest features safely is often completely dependent on the ability to test for features easily and adjust your approach accordingly. There's no way for even the most obsessive developer to know which browser supports which features on what platform, and there's no way to know what the future holds for features and browser support. You have to rely on a system to manage the use of Open Web Platform features. Feature detection is that system.

Feature detection itself has gotten more complicated. In many cases the basic pattern of testing directly against the presence of an object or method on the `window` or `document` still holds, but there are many places, like testing for EXIF Orientation in JPEG images, native form validation, or the `autoplay` attribute on HTML5 `video` elements, where different techniques need to be used. The breadth of different features, different implementation details, complexity of features, and plain-old browser bugs can all conspire to make your life difficult when trying to figure out whether or not a user can handle a specific feature.

Looking at a More Complicated Feature Detection

For a playful, but still instructive example, testing for native Emoji (*http://bit.ly/uw-emoji*) rendering support in browsers is more complicated than the average feature detection. Because you need to test for the full cartoon rendering of the glyph, and not just a flat character, the test fires up an instance of the Canvas 2D context to read in the Emoji character and test that a selected pixel is in color:

```
function testEmoji() {
  var node = document.createElement('canvas');
  if (!(node.getContext && node.getContext('2d'))) {
    return false;
  }
  var ctx = node.getContext('2d');
  ctx.textBaseline = "top";
  ctx.font = "32px Arial";
  //"smiling face with open mouth" emoji
  ctx.fillText('\ud83d\ude03', 0, 0);
  return ctx.getImageData(16, 16, 1, 1).data[0] != 0;
};
```

So the test for this feature (*http://bit.ly/uw-emoji-test*) runs seven lines and requires knowledge of a couple of different technologies (Canvas and Emoji themselves) to be properly crafted. There are many other web features that require the same or even a greater level of understanding. I don't care who you are, there are going to be examples of advanced feature detection that are going to be outside your area of expertise. If you run into one of those, like the three mentioned previously, or other examples, like testing for CSS Hyphens (*http://bit.ly/uw-css-hyphen*), formulating your own test can be a hairpulling experience.

Thankfully, there's an answer for that complexity in the form of Modernizr.

Using Modernizr

Modernizr allows you to simply and (mostly) efficiently test for web platform features without having to break down the individual specifications for every feature yourself.

 Modernizr Doesn't Actually Modernize Anything

Modernizr is a terrible name for this library, because it implies that the library itself "modernizes" older browsers into supporting new web technologies. This is a common misunderstanding. Although that would be *amazing*, that's not what Modernizr does. With the exception of allowing you to render HTML5 elements in older versions of Internet Explorer, Modernizr is simply a feature-detection library.

It's going to report the presence or absence of features. What you do with that information is up to you.

Let's look at what Modernizr *does* do and how you can use it to smoothly enhance the experience for users with advanced browsers while still maintaining a good browsing experience for users who might not have access to the best technology.

One of the ways that Modernizr helps with maintaining a good browsing experience specifically for users of older versions of Internet Explorer (which we can all agree isn't the best technology) is with an optional component that helps ensure that new HTML5 elements can be styled and scripted safely. This component isn't strictly related to feature detection, but it's historically been a core feature of Modernizr, and it's an important option to keep in mind if you're planning on supporting older versions of Internet Explorer. Let's learn about it.

Old IE: The One Thing Modernizr Does Modernize

There are few lines of code that have had more influence on web development than the HTML5Shiv. Back in the DHTML days, there was the "Netscape Navigator resize fix" which allowed us to experiment with the separation of content and style with semantic markup and CSS by fixing a horrible bug with absolutely positioned elements in Netscape Navigator 4 breaking when the page was resized. Macromedia even bundled the fix into Dreamweaver. It would be automatically inserted whenever you added a div to the document. It was everywhere and got us started on the path to "table-free" layouts. Still, considering the fact that HTML, CSS, and JavaScript almost died in favor of Flash after the DHTML era fizzled out, and, conversely, HTML5 has rushed to take over the planet in the past few years, I think the score is fully in the HTML5Shiv's favor.

So, what is it? The HTML5Shiv is a small script that enables the scripting and styling of HTML5 elements in older versions of Internet Explorer. Internet Explorer 8 and earlier completely ignored "unknown" elements. If you were trying to get ahead of the curve and use the `<article>` element, things were going to get weird in Internet Explorer. You couldn't style the element directly, and it was dead to the browser in the cascade. Thankfully, through a serendipitous chain of events, which you can read all about in Paul Irish's article, "The History of the HTML5 Shiv (*http://bit.ly/uw-html5-shiv/*)," it was discovered that by simply using the DOM method `document.createElement` to create a single example of any elements you wanted to use in the page, IE would happily allow you to script and style previously unknown elements. This allowed the immediate adoption of the new markup patterns well in advance of any sort of formal support in browsers and without worry about IE causing catastrophic problems.

Modernizr includes this script in most common builds. You'll learn about the different build options for Modernizr in "Customizing Modernizr" on page 80, but for now, just assume that unless you've specifically ignored it, Modernizr probably includes the HTML5Shiv, and you should be OK with using new HTML5 semantic elements, even if you have to support older versions of Internet Explorer.

Using (and Not Using) Modernizr

At its most basic level, to "use" Modernizr, you just need to include it in your page. What's more, if all you're really after is support for `<section>` and `<article>` in older versions of IE, then that's it. You're done. You don't have to write another line of code.

Now, if supporting Internet Explorer 8 and earlier is all you're really looking to do and you're not taking advantage of any of the other features Modernizr offers, it would actually be better to skip Modernizr entirely and simply use the HTML5Shiv without the Modernizr wrapper and global Modernizr object. This is something that does happen, so it's worth taking a look at this configuration.

The following sample shows what using the HTMLShiv directly would look like. By including the HTML5shiv, which is available from the project homepage (*http://bit.ly/uw-html5-shiv-use*), the text will read "green only if shivved" in a nice green color, even in IE8 and earlier. The screenshot shown in Figure 3-2 illustrates this.

The code is simple enough. An HTML5 `article` element wraps two span elements. The `span` elements have classes that show or hide and color the content based on the ability of the browser to recognize `article` in the cascade:

```
<!DOCTYPE html>
<html>
  <head>
    <meta charset="utf-8">
    <link rel="stylesheet" href="html5shiv.css">
    <!--[if lt IE 9]>
      <script src="html5shiv.js"></script>
    <![endif]-->
  </head>
  <body>
    <article>
      <h1>The Uncertain Web</h1>
      <h2><span class="shivved">Green only if </span>
      <span class="notshivved">Not </span>shivved</h2>
    </article>
  </body>
</html>
```

A simple CSS file (`html5shiv.css`, as referenced in the HTML) drives the difference. Browsers that can pick up the `article`, which includes Internet Explorer with the HTML5Shiv, hide the `notshivved` span, show the `shivved` span, and color the h2 element green (Figure 3-2):

```
h2 .shivved {
  display:none;
}
h2 .notshivved {
  display:inline;
}
article h2 .shivved{
  display:inline;
}
article h2 .notshivved {
  display:none;
}
article h2 {
  color:green;
}
```

The Uncertain Web

Green only if shivved

Figure 3-2. A screenshot with the HTML5Shiv

Without the HTM5Shiv, it shows "Not shivved" in the default black text (Figure 3-3).

The Uncertain Web

Not shivved

Figure 3-3. A screenshot without the HTML5Shiv

So, to sum up, include the script and semantic elements work in older Internet Explorer versions. It really doesn't get much easier than that.

You Might Want to Inline the HMTL5Shiv
If this is your configuration, you might want to inline the contents of the HTML5Shiv script instead of including it as a separate file. This will be slightly faster because you will not have to make the extra network request for the HTML5Shiv file.

So now that you've seen what the HTML5shiv does and when it makes sense to skip Modernizr, let's take a look at using it properly. Unless you're only using semantic elements, you're going to want to take advantage of the feature detection options it offers.

Feature Detection with Modernizr

Now that we've seen the exception, let's look at the more common case of taking advantage of what Modernizr has to offer. Let's first examine what Modernizr does to the page. It makes important changes to your document that you need to understand to fully embrace what it has to offer.

The Other Exception

It's worth pointing out that if you're only using one or two feature detections from Modernizr, it's possible to skip the library itself and just crib the feature detection logic from the project without any of the other pieces of the framework. I'm happy to leverage Modernizr because I don't want to do a ton of plumbing if I don't have to, but if you're more enterprising, it's worth keeping in the back of your mind.

The following HTML page includes the custom build of Modernizr that comes with the HTML5 Boilerplate (*http://html5boiler plate.com/*) project. It's a curated build that includes common tests. There are two things to note in this example. There's a "no-js" CSS class on the HTML element, and Modernizr is loaded in the head. If JavaScript is available, Modernizr will remove the no-js class. If it's there, it's useful because it's a CSS hint that JavaScript isn't available in the browser. Modernizr is loaded in the head, as opposed to the bottom of the body element, because it needs to perform its tests as soon as possible, in order to, among other things, avoid a flash of unstyled content (FOUC) (*http://bit.ly/uw-fouc*) and provide the earliest warning that certain features aren't available:

```
<!DOCTYPE html>
<html class="no-js">
  <head>
    <meta charset="utf-8">
    <script
      src="../_assets/js/vendor/modernizr-2.7.1.min.js">
    </script>
  </head>
  <body>
    <h1>The Uncertain Web</h1>
  </body>
</html>
```

So what happens when it runs? Here's the same page transformed by Modernizr when run in Google Chrome. Note the CSS classes on the

HTML element. Each of these classes represents the positive result of a Modernizr test, indicating, with a CSS class, that the feature is available:

```
<html class=" js flexbox canvas canvastext webgl touch
geolocation postmessage websqldatabase indexeddb hashchange
history draganddrop websockets rgba hsla multiplebgs
backgroundsize borderimage borderradius boxshadow textshadow
opacity cssanimations csscolumns cssgradients cssreflections
csstransforms csstransforms3d csstransitions fontface
generatedcontent video audio localstorage sessionstorage
webworkers applicationcache svg inlinesvg smil svgclippaths"
style="">
  <head>
    <meta charset="utf-8">
    <script
      src="../_assets/js/vendor/modernizr-2.7.1.min.js">
    </script>
  </head>
  <body style="">
    <h1>The Uncertain Web</h1>
  </body>
</html>
```

Here's the same document after running in Internet Explorer 7. As you can see, the prefix "no-" is attached to the majority of the classes, indicating a series of failing tests:

```
<html class=" js no-flexbox no-canvas no-canvastext no-webgl
no-touch no-geolocation postmessage no-websqldatabase
no-indexeddb no-hashchange no-history draganddrop no-websockets
no-rgba no-hsla no-multiplebgs no-backgroundsize no-borderimage
no-borderradius no-boxshadow no-textshadow no-opacity
no-cssanimations no-csscolumns no-cssgradients no-cssreflections
no-csstransforms no-csstransforms3d no-csstransitions fontface
no-generatedcontent no-video no-audio no-localstorage
no-sessionstorage no-webworkers no-applicationcache no-svg
no-inlinesvg no-smil no-svgclippaths">
  <head>
    <meta charset="utf-8">
    <script
      src="../_assets/js/vendor/modernizr-2.7.1.min.js">
    </script>
  </head>
  <body style="">
    <h1>The Uncertain Web</h1>
  </body>
</html>
```

Modernizr also creates a Modernizr object in the global JavaScript namespace, which in addition to several other methods and properties that you'll learn about in "Additional Modernizr Methods" on page 86, offers a Boolean test for each of the tested features. The following code sample outputs the full set of tests in this custom build:

```html
<!DOCTYPE html>
<html>
  <head>
    <meta charset-"utf-8">
    <script
      src="../_assets/js/vendor/modernizr-2.7.1.min.js">
    </script>
  </head>
  <body>
    <h1>The Uncertain Web</h1>
    <script>
      for (var prop in Modernizr){
        console.log(prop+": "+ Modernizr[prop])
      }
    </script>
  </body>
</html>
```

The output of the console is visible in Figure 3-4. Chrome, the browser in this example, supports all of the tested features.

Figure 3-4. Console output showing the result of Modernizr tests in Google Chrome

This information can be used in a couple of different ways. These tests can be used to fork code, just like we did when testing for docu ment.getElementById back in the DHTML era, or you can use these tests to alternatively load a polyfill solution for the missing feature.

Before we review in depth how to use the tests, let's look at how you can get your hands on a copy of Modernizr that makes sense for you.

Customizing Modernizr

There are two ways you're going to use Modernizr. You will want to have a version for development and one version for production. For development, you could use the custom build in HTML5 Boilerplate, as I've done here, or the development version that Modernizr itself provides, which includes all of their core tests for development (*http:// bit.ly/uw-modernizr-dev*). Having all of these tests run every time incurs a slight performance penalty, but for development, it's useful to be able to test quickly against a feature without having to adjust your build of the library. On the other hand, for production, you'd want to include tests for just the features you're going to use in order to speed up the loading of your site.

For example, if you're working with SVG and need to work with older versions of Internet Explorer or the Android browser, you would create a custom build that includes the HTML5Shiv (for older IE) and the test for SVG. You can do this on the Modernizr download page (*http://modernizr.com/download/*).

The builder is pretty easy to use. Simply select your features (Figure 3-5) and download your custom copy.

Figure 3-5. Downloading a custom copy of Modernizr

Now that you know how to get a custom version that includes just the tests you need, let's put it to use.

Using Modernizr's Tests

This section will show you how to use the Modernizr tests in three different ways:

- Using the CSS classes
- Using the Modernizr object to test against specific properties and fork your code
- Using the Modernizr object to test and load a polyfill solution

Using the Modernizr CSS classes is very straightforward. As the following example shows, you can easily use the svg class on the HTML element to style the markup on your page. In this case, you will conditionally load/not load an SVG image in the background of a div element. If Modernizr finds SVG support and places the svg class on the HTML element, then the background of the div will be an SVG image. Otherwise, without SVG support, it's going to be a PNG. Although older browsers won't get the potential scaling or size benefits of an SVG image, they will get a background image. Nothing breaks.

Newer browsers get all the benefits of SVG. Modernizr makes this easy. Here's how it's done:

```
<!DOCTYPE html>
<html>
  <head>
    <meta charset="utf-8">
    <script src="modernizr.custom.52324.js">
        </script>
    <style type="text/css">
      .HTML5 {
        width: 600px;
        height:650px;
        background-position: center bottom;
        background-repeat: no-repeat;
        text-align: center;
      }
      .svg .HTML5 {
        background-image:url(HTML5-logo.svg);
      }
      .no-svg .HTML5 {
        background-image:url(HTML5_Logo_512.png);
      }
    </style>
  </head>
  <body>
    <h1>The Uncertain Web</h1>
    <div class="HTML5"><h2>HTML5 is the best</h2></div>
  </body>
</html>
```

Similarly, using the Modernizr object to test for browser features in JavaScript is pretty easy as well. As the following code sample shows, as soon as you load your custom version of Modernizr, the Modern izr.svg test is available. In this sample, the Modernizr.svg property is used to conditionally insert an SVG element into the page and bind a jQuery event to the circle element, which changes its fill color from hot pink to a very corporate blue on click. If SVG isn't available, then an img element is inserted into the document, and a click handler is attached, which changes its src to a blue image:

```
<!DOCTYPE html>
<html>
  <head>
    <meta charset="utf-8">
    <script
      src="modernizr.custom.52324.js">
    </script>
  </head>
```

```
<body>
  <h1>The Uncertain Web</h1>
  <div id="svg"></div>
  <script src="../_assets/js/vendor/jquery-1.11.0.min.js">
  </script>
  <script>
  $(document).ready(function(){
    if (Modernizr.svg){
      $("#svg").load("circle.svg");
      $("#svg").on("click","circle",function(){
        $(this).attr("fill","#003366")
      })
    } else {
      $("#svg").append("<img src='circle.png'>");
       $("#svg img").on("click",function(){
        $(this).attr("src","circle-blue.png")
      })
    }
  })
  </script>
</body>
</html>
```

Finally, the Modernizr object can be used to test against web platform features, and using the optional Modernizr.load (*http://bit.ly/uw-modernizr-load*) utility (or your script loader of choice), load polyfills scripts to fill in functionality for older browsers. In this example, there is a custom build of Modernizr (*http://bit.ly/uw-mod-custom*) that includes a test for the `input` element's `placeholder` attribute. Using `Modernizr.load` to test against `Modernizr.placeholder`, a polyfill called Placeholders.js (*http://bit.ly/uw-placeholders*) is loaded if the test fails:

```
<!DOCTYPE html>
<html>
  <head>
    <meta charset="utf-8">
    <script src="modernizr.custom.42574.js"></script>
    <script>
    Modernizr.load({
      test: Modernizr.placeholder,
      nope: 'placeholders.min.js'
    });
    </script>
  </head>
  <body>
    <h1>The Uncertain Web</h1>
    <form>
      <div>
        <label for="text">Placeholder:
```

```
  <input type="text"
    placeholder="This is example text"></label>
  </div>
  </form>
  </body>
  </html>
```

You're not required to use Modernizr.load, of course. It's actually being pulled out of the core build of Modernizr (*http://bit.ly/uw-modernizr-load-pulled*) for version 3.0 (which feels like it's been ready to drop *any day* for two years now). You can use any script-loading solution you like, including just using document.write to insert the script tag into the page. Whatever tool you use, the pattern remains basically the same. Test for the feature, and if the test fails, insert the polyfill script.

These three different examples represent the common ways you'll use Modernizr.

The benefits and drawbacks of the polyfill option are important to grasp, so let's take a look at the general topic of polyfills in a little bit more detail.

Cross Browser Polyfills

One of the best, somewhat unsung, parts of the Modernizr project is the collection of HTML5 Cross Browser Polyfills (*http://bit.ly/uw-html5-cbp*) that the community maintains on the project wiki. If you're looking to use a new CSS, HTML, or JavaScript feature, there's a chance that you can find a polyfill for the feature on the Modernizr wiki. This is invaluable. Polyfills have allowed us to move forward with new technologies without leaving older browsers behind. This, like the HTML5Shiv, has allowed HTML5 to grow and prosper much faster than anyone initially expected. Several, like the one for the humble placeholder attribute you saw in the previous section, or the not-so-humble Flash and VML-based polyfills for SVG and Canvas support in older versions of IE, have been standard options for me for years. I couldn't have gotten by without tools like FlashCanvas (*http://flash canvas.net/*), a flash-based Canvas polyfill, or Raphaël, an SVG-authoring library that automatically polyfills for SVG in older versions of Internet Explorer. They've been great to work with and have allowed us to do things we couldn't have done otherwise, without shutting out 10–40% of our audience.

There is a potential dark side, however. Polyfills, depending on the underlying technology used to create the fallback feature, can at times be more trouble than they're worth. Performance, maintenance, and bug fixing are all made harder with a dependency on polyfills. The issues that arise are illustrated perfectly in this Stack Overflow answer from Jason Johnston, the creator of the CSS3 Pie (*http://css3pie.com/*) project, to the question "Why are CSS3 PIE and other similar scripts not in use everywhere?" (*http://bit.ly/uw-johnston-css3pie*) CSS3Pie, a polyfill for CSS3 features in Internet Explorer, is an ingenious piece of code that delights people when they first encounter it. It also has a deserved reputation for performance issues:

1. They do incur a certain performance cost. CSS3 PIE in particular starts to create a noticeable rendering delay after use on about two dozen elements (in my experience, YMMV.) For that reason its use on large pages might cause a larger rendering delay than the time saved downloading image assets.

2. They start to show bugs with complex DOM changes. Lots of animation, showing/hiding, etc. can sometimes cause PIE to get out of sync.

3. Related to #2, the added layer of abstraction (and its associated bugs) can become a detriment on large development teams with a complex codebase. If you start spending more time debugging the abstraction than it would take to simply create rounded corner images, then the tool is getting in the way.

> — Stack Overflow user lojjic
> *Stack Overflow Question: Why are CSS3 PIE and other similar*
> *scripts not in use everywhere?*

So when you're trying to look at the technology stack for your application and are looking to use some cutting-edge options, keep the polyfill option in mind. Modernizr makes it easy to conditionally load resources, so take advantage of that. Also, just because it's easy doesn't mean you have to do it. There are plenty of opportunities to replace certain features or let certain design elements, like rounded corners (to pick my favorite example), degrade in older browsers. It takes some care, but it's possible to balance the developer ergonomics that Modernizr and polyfills provide with user experience goals and frontend performance.

Additional Modernizr Methods

In addition to the core tests, Modernizr also offers some utilities and extensibility options that help manage the minefield of modern development.

Modernizr.prefixed()

Vendor or browser prefixes are string prefixes (e.g., -webkit- or -moz-) to CSS properties that, theoretically, allow browsers to experiment with features but still retain the ability to change their mind about implementation details before the feature is finalized. It didn't really work out that way in practice (*http://bit.ly/uw-vendor-prefix*). What's worse is they're still something to manage in your code. In CSS, they are relatively easy to deal with, as you can just stack the properties, and the browser will understand the one that it's meant to read:

```
.box_scale {
    -webkit-transform: scale(0.8);   /* Chrome, Safari 3.1+ */
      -moz-transform: scale(0.8);   /* Firefox 3.5+ */
       -ms-transform: scale(0.8);   /* IE 9 */
        -o-transform: scale(0.8);   /* Opera 10.50-12.00 */
           transform: scale(0.8);   /* Standard! */
}
```

CSS preprocessors, like SASS and LESS, make this easy, but even writing CSS by hand is not too much of a hardship, especially if you write one class for certain effects and then apply them as needed to individual elements.

In JavaScript, things are less straightforward because you'd have to actually test against every possibility, every time you wanted to adjust one of the potentially prefixed features. You can work around this by liberal use of predefined CSS classes or maybe writing CSS classes into a style element on the fly, but none of those options are as flexible as being able to directly manipulate properties of the element's style object. Modernizr.prefixed() allows you do to this. This method returns the correct (prefixed or nonprefixed) property name variant of your input for the current browser. To use it, you simply call Modernizr.prefixed with the target property as an argument and use that result in bracket notation to look up the required property:

```
$('#elem').on("click",function() {
    var transform = 'scale(0.8)';
    this.style[Modernizr.prefixed('transform')] = transform;
});
```

`Modernizr.prefixed` also allows you to find prefixed DOM properties and methods by passing in a second argument. For example, passing in `requestAnimationFrame` as the targeted method and `window` as the object to search through, would return DOM method wrapped in `raf` in supporting browsers:

```
window.raf = Modernizr.prefixed('requestAnimationFrame', window)
  || function( callback ){
  window.setTimeout(callback, 1000 / 60);
}
```

As you can see, this is a nice, clean way to work around the inconvenience of browser prefixes.

Modernizr.mq()

`Modernizr.mq` provides a JavaScript method to test a given media query against the current state of the document. It's available as an option on the download page.

For example, the following test queries, for all media, whether or not the page is at the `max-width` of `768px`, and on page load and resize, writes the result of the test to the screen:

```html
<!DOCTYPE html>
<html>
  <head>
    <meta charset="utf-8">
    <script src="modernizr.custom.05753.js"></script>
  </head>
  <body>
    <h1>The Uncertain Web</h1>
    <h2></h2>
    <script
      src="../_assets/js/vendor/jquery-1.10.2.min.js">
    </script>
    <script>
      function maxWidthtest(){
        if (Modernizr.mq('all and (max-width: 768px)')){
          $("h2").text("less than 768px");
        } else {
          $("h2").text("greater than 768px");
        }
      }
      $(document).ready(maxWidthtest);
      $(window).on("resize",maxWidthtest);
    </script>
  </body>
</html>
```

`Modernizr.mq` also allows you to test for media query support. Using a combination of Modernizr.load and Modernizr.mq would allow you to conditionally load respond.js (*http://bit.ly/uw-respondjs*), a media query polyfill library:

```
<!DOCTYPE html>
<html>
  <head>
    <meta charset="utf-8">
    <script src="modernizr.custom.05753.js"></script>
    <script>
      Modernizr.load({
        test: Modernizr.mq("only all"),
        nope: "respond.min.js"
      });
    </script>
  </head>
  <body>
    <h1>The Uncertain Web</h1>
  </body>
</html>
```

This is a nice feature when working on responsive sites, as you can use the same vocabulary throughout development to identify breakpoints.

Managing the Undetectables

There are certain web features that aren't detectable by Modernizr. There's even a Modernizr wiki page dedicated to them (*http://bit.ly/ uw-undetectables*). There can be different reasons for this. Performance can be one. Doing some of the `video` and `audio` element tests, for example, would require loading a video or audio file. That's really not feasible to test before the end of the `head` of the document. Others are blocked by no clear implementation hook to test against, like the `color` and `date` input types. Still others are blocked by buggy implementations. You can test against the presence of the object, but if the feature doesn't behave the ways it's expected to behave, then the test is useless.

This last issue creeps into (mostly) reliable tests as well. For example the `@font-face` test includes a user agent blacklist (*http://bit.ly/uw-user-agent-blacklist*) that improves the fidelity of the Modernizr test by returning false for known problem browsers.

There are also certain web features that aren't so much impossible to test as they are impossible to conceptualize a thing to test for. There's a lot of discussion on the Modernizr repo (*http://bit.ly/uw-modernizr-touch*) about how to reliably test for a user with a touchscreen device. Part of this is due to the poorly named `Modernizr.touch` test, which is actually a simple test for the presence of the touch* family of events. They'll be renamed to `Modernizr.touchevents` moving forward, which will help somewhat, but what people want out of Modernizr here is clearly a test that tells them whether or not the user is a "mouse" user or a "touch" user. The answer to this question is so complicated that smoke basically pours out of people's heads when they start to think about it. If someone were to observe my behavior as I type these words, they would find it difficult to pinpoint what kind of user I am. I'm on a Windows 8 laptop with a touchscreen and a trackpad. I use both, all the time. Am I a mouse user? A touch user? I've been known to add a pen and drawing tablet to the device as well. What am I then? A pen user? If you can't hope to answer it watching me with human eyes, then what hope do you have with JavaScript? Even if the question "Can this user ever use a touchscreen?" can be answered, it might not be the right question to ask. This particular issue is so large it will be covered in detail in Chapter 5.

Generally, dealing with undetectable features can be handled in a few different ways.

You can browser sniff

Back in the day, I would commonly sniff for IE6 using IE's conditional comments (*http://bit.ly/uw-conditional-comments*) when working with 32-bit PNGs. I would simply swap out the PNG for a transparent GIF with CSS. This isn't foolproof, especially because using the user agent string for browser sniffing isn't as precise as using conditional comments (which themselves are gone in Internet Explorer 11 on), but it's sometimes all you can do.

You can limit your use of these features to safe implementations

Basically, if you can shrug if the feature fails, then go ahead and use it. The `date` input is a good example of this. If it's supported, you get a fancy date picker. If it's not supported, it falls back to being a regular text input. As long as you validate the date the user enters, you'll be fine either way.

Design robust systems that work in many different configurations

Don't rely on any specific configuration. The touch versus mouse example will illustrate this in depth in Chapter 5, as do the image and video markup patterns seen in Chapters 6 and 7. In general, the idea is to always choose code patterns that allow your site to function in legacy browsers. In the case of touch and mouse input, that means ensuring you're binding events to both touch and mouse events. With the embedded media, that means that you provide fallback markup and media formats for older browsers. Whatever technology you're using, the goal should be to provide something functional for everyone that visits your site.

As you can probably guess, this concept will be covered throughout the rest of the book.

Forgo the feature entirely

You may just have to skip over the feature entirely in order to ensure that every user gets a usable experience. A `color` picker might be the best example of this. If you're expecting a user to be able to enter a color, and you need to support the widest possible browser palette, then you might have to skip the native color picker and go directly to a JavaScript library that provides the same functionality. Expecting the average user to be able to spit out a hex value into a text box is unrealistic, so you need to ensure that the user has the ability to pick from a full spectrum palette.

Handling undetectables with grace is one of the cornerstones of the uncertain Web. Sometimes you truly can't know about a certain feature. Accepting that and solving the problem in a way that might not be binary, but is the best possible solution for the broadest number of your users is one of the concepts you need to take to heart to be successful on today's Web.

Common Feature Tests and Associated Polyfills

This section examines some of the most common features to test for with notes on how these tests might fit into your own development. These were identified as the 10 most popular features from the Modernizr custom builder (*http://bit.ly/uw-modernizr-top*). I've grouped several thematically because the way I approach each group is similar.

Modernizr.touch

That this is the number one test for Modernizr users is validation that I've written the right book. You've already learned a little bit about the complexity of this issue, and you'll learn much more about this issue in Chapter 5. For now, I'll leave you with this warning from the Modernizr source: "[Modernizr.touch] indicates if the browser supports the Touch Events spec, and does not necessarily reflect a touchscreen device."

Modernizr.input

That this test is the second most popular is heartening to me, as I've always felt that the new HTML5 form enhancements were neglected by the development community in favor of sexier additions to the web platform, like Canvas and Web Sockets. This test is actually an object that exposes the following individual tests representing new HTML5 input attributes:

- `Modernizr.input.autocomplete`
- `Modernizr.input.autofocus`
- `Modernizr.input.list`
- `Modernizr.input.max`
- `Modernizr.input.min`
- `Modernizr.input.multiple`
- `Modernizr.input.pattern`
- `Modernizr.input.placeholder`
- `Modernizr.input.required`
- `Modernizr.input.step`

There are plenty of polyfill solutions (*http://bit.ly/uw-polyfill-solutions*) available for these attributes. You've already seen `place holder` in action (albeit with the standalone placeholder test) already.

Personally, I most often end up using a subset of these tests in concert with other libraries or frameworks. I might use the `placeholder` test to polyfill for the `placeholder` attribute, but I would use AngularJS's built-in form validation tools rather than relying on `Modernizr.input.required` and a polyfill.

Modernizr.csstransitions, Modernizr.csstransforms3d, and Modernizr.csstransforms

These three are an interesting case. Beyond being some of the most interesting work being done in the CSS specification space, they've also generated some of the greatest CSS demos of the past few years. In the context of the uncertain Web, they're also interesting because they are a technology that I have zero faith in but will always leverage where possible. Modernizr helps do that. For people with supporting browsers, being able to leverage these new CSS3 technologies can really help polish an experience, and in many cases, you can easily create a decent fallback experience for people with browsers that can't keep up.

Modernizr.inputtypes

Like `Modernizr.input`, this test exposes an object featuring tests for many of the new `input` types. The list is as follows:

- `Modernizr.inputtypes.color`
- `Modernizr.inputtypes.date`
- `Modernizr.inputtypes.datetime`
- `Modernizr.inputtypes[datetime-local]`
- `Modernizr.inputtypes.email`
- `Modernizr.inputtypes.month`
- `Modernizr.inputtypes.number`
- `Modernizr.inputtypes.range`
- `Modernizr.inputtypes.search`
- `Modernizr.inputtypes.tel`
- `Modernizr.inputtypes.time`
- `Modernizr.inputtypes.url`
- `Modernizr.inputtypes.week`

Pesonally, with the exception of the input types that would throw up a native datepicker in supporting browsers (date, datetime, datetime-local, month, time), I don't actually worry about whether or not a browser can support `email` or `url` as an `input` type. At the end of the day, these input types will fall back to acting like text inputs, so there's no danger in presenting them to your users—as long as you're validating your inputs.

For those inputs that would activate the native datepicker, I will either use the tests and will polyfill with a stack suitable polyfill (e.g., jQuery UI (*http://bit.ly/uw-datepicker*) on a jQuery project or Bootstrap Datepicker (*http://bit.ly/uw-bootstrap-datepicker*) on a Twitter Bootstrap project) or will forgo native altogether and just use the library code to have a single experience to manage.

Modernizr.canvas and Modernizr.svg

If you're going to use SVG or the Canvas 2D API in any way that matters, you should have a plan for how to deal with browsers that don't support these technologies. Because of that, these tests are invaluable.

Most of the time, I use static content for older browsers. Charts, for example, can often be generated automatically as part of a build process or on the server side and served as a JPG or PNG. It's a more stable approach, and you're not overloading an older browser with a polyfill technology that might tax its JavaScript engine.

That said, if the content needs to be dynamic, using these tests can allow you to easily serve up polyfill solutions. For pure polyfill solutions, I've had success with SVGWeb (*http://bit.ly/uw-svgweb*) for SVG and FlashCanvas (*http://flashcanvas.net/*) for Canvas. I was especially surprised by how well FlashCanvas handled the majority of what we threw at it. These solutions are, by nature, limited. Even when they're actively maintained (as FlashCanvas is), they're always going to be behind the specifications and the browser vendors, so if you can, look toward leveraging static content.

This is especially important with SVG because there is no polyfill solution for SVG in Android 2.3 and older.

Modernizr.fontface

This is an especially important test for those of you looking to leverage one of the many font icon sets out there like Font Awesome (*http://bit.ly/uw-font-awesome*). If you don't have decent CSS fallbacks for browsers that don't support `@font-face`, you can really degrade the appearance and usability of your site.

Personally, I've never warmed to icon fonts for just that reason, but they are appealing to many people, so this test is very important.

Modernizr.video

As you'll see in Chapter 7 where I discuss video in depth, I don't like to handle video myself. My preference is to leverage a company that does video for a living (YouTube, Vimeo, Brightcove, etc.) and let the experts handle all the complexity of web video. Even if you're looking to go it alone, Chapter 7 will show you a different cross-browser approach that doesn't need this test.

"Frontend Development Done Right"

Modernizr and feature detection are cornerstones of your web development toolbox. Being able to quickly add tests for web platform features allows you to craft fallback solutions without too much trouble. Whether you're using a polyfill solution, wholly alternative content, or forgoing features entirely, the JavaScript and CSS tests that Modernizr provides are invaluable when you're working on today's Web. Using the CSS classes and the tests available in the `Modernizr` JavaScript object, you can easily fork your code to handle edge cases or conditionally load polyfills for older browsers. Modernizr allows you to customize builds to include just the tests and tools you need for your application. Modernizr also offers utilities for developing with vendor prefixes and media queries in JavaScript.

Hopefully, this chapter will set you on the path to, as the Modernizr folks say of their library, "frontend development done right."

CHAPTER 4

Selecting Responsive Design or Another Mobile Experience

The control which designers know in the print medium, and often
desire in the web medium, is simply a function of the limitation of
the printed page. We should embrace the fact that the web doesn't
have the same constraints, and design for this flexibility.
But first, we must accept the ebb and flow of things.

— John Allsopp

One of the places where embracing uncertainty matters most and is
most readily apparent to developers and designers is deciding how to
handle the full depth of devices and screen resolutions out there. Users
expect to be able get to your content and data with any device they've
got in their hands. How you satisfy that multiscreen requirement is a
major question facing any project these days. Balancing the desire for
beautiful designs, world-class usability, top performance, and the
maintainability of your platform are all factors that are going to come
into play.

I stole the above quote (*http://bit.ly/uw-dao*). Well, I didn't *steal* it so
much as copy its use as the lead-in to some writing about responsive
web design (RWD). It's a few sentences that capture the very heart of
the Web that I want—a flexible, universal medium. That sort of thinking embraces the Web in ways that I completely endorse. It's also 14
years old.

So, where did I crib it from? It's the quote that introduces the article
that introduced RWD to the world.

That article appeared on May 25, 2010, when Ethan Marcotte published the directly named "Responsive Web Design" (*http://bit.ly/uw-rwd*) on A List Apart. In the article, he outlined the conceptual and technical framework of RWD, namely using fluid layout grids and CSS3 media queries (*http://bit.ly/uw-css3-media*) to create layouts that could adapt and respond to the characteristics of the device or user agent—stretching and shrinking to present layouts that worked on a variety of screen sizes without prior knowledge of the device characteristics.

Around this time, projects like jQTouch (*http://jqtjs.com/*), jQuery Mobile (*http://jquerymobile.com/*), and Sencha Touch (*http://bit.ly/uw-sencha-touch*) were coming online and providing tools to produce mobile-specific sites. The ability to serve content for small screens with one codebase was an attractive alternative to creating a mobile site at *m.example.com* with a new, mobile-specific codebase.

The article made quite a stir. It was an elegant solution that leveraged just CSS, which made it accessible to the full frontend development spectrum—from hybrid designer/developers (with little or no Java-Script) all the way to full stack developers. People were rightly excited by the concept, as even at that point, the question of how to handle mobile devices was a hot topic.

As you'll see in the next section, one year later, RWD's place in the web development and design landscape was solidified beyond reproach.

In this chapter, I'll share what I've learned about RWD over the past few years and will share lessons from the Web at large in order to give you the proper perspective to make the decisions on how to architect your site or application. It will focus on the place for responsive design techniques in the uncertain Web toolbox, examining use cases where it absolutely makes sense, where it doesn't, and where you might have to flip a coin to decide which way to go. You will also learn some techniques to leverage on both sides of the responsive/mobile site divide.

Boston Globe's RWD Redesign

When my local paper, *The Boston Globe*, relaunched its site Boston-Globe.com (*http://bostonglobe.com/*) in September of 2011, it signaled the arrival of RWD as a viable technique for web design and development at the highest level. Up until that point, the excitement for the techniques hadn't really been matched by a site that proved the effectiveness of RWD at scale. The site, designed with the help of the Filament Group (*http://filamentgroup.com/*) and design agency Upstatement (*http://upstatement.com/*), was a polished, cleanly implemented site that worked well on everything from the desktop to a brand new iPad to an old Apple Newton, according to Mat Marquis (*http://twitter.com/wilto*).

In Figure 4-1, you can see the site in action. On the left, you see a desktop view. On the right, you see the small-screen view.

Figure 4-1. BostonGlobe.com in desktop and small-screen views

It made quite a splash. In web development circles, it was basically the only topic for a couple of days, and even several years later, the project remains a landmark, constantly referenced when the evolution of RWD is discussed. The folks involved have widely shared their experience and expertise in blog posts, conference talks, and interviews, further cementing the influence of the project. Even now, both the Filament Group and Upstatement still feature the project prominently on their sites.

Of course, it being a website (and therefore on the Web), everyone else also joined in the discussion, sharing their opinions of the technique, the specific implementation, and the visual design.

Really? RWD for Every Site?

One reaction in particular was actually the origin of this book. If you're a comic book guy like me, you can imagine the bat that crashes through the window in the classic *Batman* origin story giving him the idea to "become a bat." This was like that, except about websites and not at all scary (see Figure 4-2). On Twitter and in real life, people stated, without hesitation, that one day *everything* would be responsive.

Rob Larsen after Bob Kane

Figure 4-2. A dramatic re-creation of the origin of this book

Unless you jumped into this book starting from this chapter (if so, welcome!), then you know how skeptical I was toward the idea that one day everything would become responsive. Even then, I was wary of anything that seemed like a magical solution, and seeing several normally sober voices proclaim that responsive is "the one true way," clarified something that had been floating around in my head for a decade—that there's no "one true way." There's only the best way for the project you're currently on. The next project might need the same tools or approach. It might not.

Which isn't to say that I'm down on RWD in general. I'm not. I'm a fan of RWD and have built several sites, including three (*http://htmlcssjavascript.com/*) of my (*http://javaplusplusplus.com/*) own (*http://itsalljustcomics.com/*), with it. RWD is a clever solution to a big problem, and because the core concept is so simple, it allows for lots of room to experiment. But, ask yourself, do you think there's any one-size-fits-all solution? The reality is that nothing is a one-size-fits-all solution for the Web. The Web wasn't built that way. For my part, even in 2011, I'd already done enough small-screen development to recognize situations where responsive techniques were going to fall short of the requirements I was looking to meet.

For a specific example, a project I was working on at the time used a force-directed layout (*http://bit.ly/uw-force-directed*) to display the relationships between potentially many dozens of users. Even before we built it, it didn't take a soothsayer to figure out that it was going to be difficult to interact with on a small screen. For one thing, at certain resolutions, even if the visualization scaled, the text was so small as to be a form of torture. Additionally, to accommodate dozens of elements on the screen, the nodes themselves had to be pretty small, so interacting with each node was going to be a problem for the user on smaller screen devices.

Figure 4-3 shows the difficulty of interacting with one of the nodes with a finger (and not a particularly fat one, if I do say so myself). This photo is taken on a large-screen phone, the Galaxy Note II, which measures 5.95 inches (151.1 mm) × 3.17 inches (80.5 mm). Even on the Note, the text is difficult to read in Portrait mode.

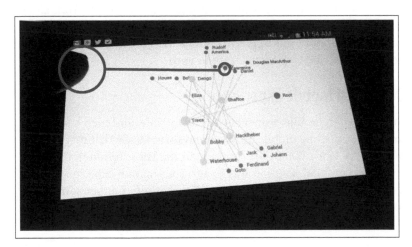

Figure 4-3. A comparison of the author's thumb and a single node in a force-directed graph

The years since the launch of *The Boston Globe* site have only cemented this opinion. Considering the amount of work I've done with data grids (*http://bit.ly/uw-data-grids*) and on other complex applications, it's been made clear to me that there's a case to be made for completely different interfaces, depending on design goals, application requirements, and on the class of device the user is using. There are many situations where a dedicated mobile site or some hybrid approach is by far the best choice if you have the skills and resources to execute one. For example, financial sites might have widely different use cases for mobile and desktop users. With complicated financial data, mobile users are often solely consumers of data—often in the form of reports, simple approval workflows, or visualizations—and the real work is done on the desktop.

Mobile First, RESS, and the Rest of the Mobile Development Universe

Before we get deeper into the discussion of RWD, let's take a minute to look at some of the other approaches in this space. As you'll learn in this section, there are some other concepts in this space like responsive web design with server-side components (RESS) and "mobile first." None of them really has the same footprint in developers' minds that RWD does, so it's worth discussing what they are and how they might play into this discussion. Techniques and concepts from all of these are going to fit well in the toolbox for developing modern, compatible sites—you want as many options as you can get. Whether or not you subscribe to the *label* is up to you.

Dedicated Mobile Experience

Initially, when mobile browsers were all terrible, and then later when there was only one mobile browser and form factor that mattered to people (the latest iOS Safari running on the latest iPhone), the most common "mobile" solution was to serve a separate experience optimized for mobile devices. This manifested itself as either something so dumbed down that it would run on anything that could access the Web, or something slick, yet designed to work only on the iPhone.

iphone.example.com

As an aside, the prevalence of iPhone-crafted sites created an unfortunate web development pattern. As people started to open up their mobile sites to work with Android (both browsers were based on WebKit, after all) and then general mobile browsers, they kept serving content from URLs like *http:// bookstore.umanitoba.ca/iPhone/iHome.aspx* with iPhone clearly identified in the URL (not to mention the Apple style "iHome" in the filename). There's no reason a website should expose a target platform in its URL structure.

This is accomplished with some sort of redirection based on the user agent. This can be a simple server or client-side test against the user agent string ("iPhone," "iPad," or "Android"), or a more complex query using a service like DeviceAtlas (*https://deviceatlas.com/*), or a Device Description Repository (DDR) like the Wireless Universal Resource FiLe (WURFL) (*http://bit.ly/uw-wurfl*), or OpenDDR (*http:// www.openddr.org/*), which uses the user agent string and a dedicated database to return information about the device's characteristics. Microsoft has even built this capability into its .Net MVC framework. The framework can do server-side device detection and then shows the best view based on what type of device it detects.

As you'll soon see, a more nuanced approach to a dedicated mobile experience that is more flexible in layout (often leveraging RWD techniques) and doesn't tie itself to any specific device is still very common, especially with the largest sites on the Internet.

Mobile First

Mobile first is exactly what the name implies, designing and developing the mobile experience first and then potentially working on enhancements for the desktop experience. This concept ties closely with the concept of progressive enhancement.

Mobile First is also the title of a book by Luke Wroblewski, one of the people you should be following if you're interested in this conversation.

Progressive Enhancement

Progressive enhancement is an old stalwart of web development. The basic concept of progressive enhancement is to create a widely compatible baseline solution and then add on features and functionality, depending on available browser features. It differs from mobile first in that progressive enhancement can also be part of a desktop first approach to web development.

RESS

I'm not sure how well this acronym will catch on, but it does come up, so here it is. With REsponsive web design with ServerSide components (RESS), Luke Wroblewski (*I told you he was someone to pay attention to*) attempts to define a hybrid pattern that leverages the server side to render some elements of a single codebase, depending on the device class.

I don't like the acronym personally, because to me it immediately evokes CSS preprocessors like Compass, SASS, and LESS rather than RWD. This isn't a fatal flaw, I guess, but for me it just feels off, and I never took to using it. *Also, where are the W, D, and C?*

His advocacy of hybrid solutions is, however, a useful foil to the folks that seem to have a philosophical aversion to leveraging the server. To my mind, not taking advantage of the server in web development is silly, and he understands this completely. Purity in approach doesn't win you points with your users. Giving them the best possible experience does.

Microsoft's .Net MVC is geared toward using this type of approach.

Choosing a Development Path

So, if you're not going to just make every site responsive, then what are you going to do instead?

You're going to make the best possible decision for your project.

You've got options. The basic spectrum has a fully responsive site (with one codebase) that responds to the device's capabilities on one end, and then dedicated mobile and desktop experiences with two separate, dedicated codebases on the other. Somewhere in the middle might be a RESS solution. Nothing on the Web is truly black and white. Your site can end up anywhere on that spectrum.

This section is going to focus on preparing you for the choice.

What you do is going to be decided on a few factors. The following sections outline some of the more common factors that will influence your decision.

The Size and Skills of Your Team

If you're a lone developer who knows nothing about the server beyond installing WordPress or Drupal from a web host's control panel, then you're probably going to want to use responsive techniques. Unless you've always wanted to learn about PHP and Apache or C# and IIS, then you're going to be much happier sticking to the tools you already know. On the other hand, if you're a strong full stack developer or have a larger team with more specialization, then more options open up for you in terms of using the server. Take advantage of them.

The Requirements of Your Site or Application

As we've already started to explore, the nature of your site or application is going to be a major determining factor for your approach. On the one hand, if you are building a pure content (text and images) site (as many of the first wave of responsive sites were), then responsive is going to be a good fit. In addition to the existing body of knowledge you can tap into to get tips and tricks, pure text and images lend themselves to RWD because it's easier to resize boxes than it is to re-work interactions. On the other hand, if you're building a more complicated application, then you may need to create an entirely different approach for small screens.

Your Demographics

As we discussed in Chapter 2, understanding your audience is key to knowing what to build.

For example, learning that your audience is increasingly visiting your site on small-screen mobile devices might mean you create a mobile-first design and then use RWD or progressive enhancement to enhance the experience of desktop or other large-screen users.

Alternatively, if you find you're doing well with immersive desktop experiences (*http://bit.ly/uw-immersive*), you may want to ramp up the experience on large screens and provide a mightily scaled-down version on a dedicated mobile site.

Your Budget

If you've got a budget, you've got even more options. I'm not talking about bringing in consultants or simply paying your own employees to solve more complex tasks. You *can* do that, but the more interesting benefit is that you can leverage solutions from software as a service (SAAS) providers, or content delivery specialists can make some thorny problems go away. Without endorsing any specific solution, a survey of some of these companies gives you a sense of what they're offering. Akamai has a white paper entitled "How To Deliver Fast, Engaging Responsive Web Design Sites" (*http://bit.ly/uw-akamai-rwd*), which, not coincidentally, includes a section entitled "Optimize Responsive Web Design Sites with Akamai." Strangeloop Networks Mobile Optimizer product promises to "Accelerate your mobile Web performance by up to 350% automatically." I can't tell you whether or not these or any similar services are going to be good for your site or application. I can't know what problems you're trying to solve. What I can tell you is that when I've had the occasion to use services like these, I've had some success, and that these services are all pay to play. You have to have at least some money to get on board.

Now that you've got a sense of what the deciding factors are and what the general landscape looks like, it's time to take a look at the drawbacks and benefits of the two ends of the spectrum, RWD and dedicated mobile experiences.

Benefits of RWD

The elevator pitch for RWD sounds like alchemy: take one codebase and handle every device and browser under the sun. With careful development, it actually does a pretty good job of delivering on that promise. The following list outlines some specific benefits of RWD.

Simplified server side

With a well-crafted responsive design, careful image usage, and an eye toward performance, you can serve one set of files with minimal server-side logic for device-specific issues to all your users.

Easier maintenance

RWD allows you to maintain one codebase for your entire frontend.

Lower overall application complexity

You can submarine this somewhat by getting too tricky on the frontend, trying to serve the perfect experience to too many users (instead
of settling for a good solution that requires less effort), but overall,
with a simpler server setup and one codebase for your frontend, you're
going to have fewer moving pieces and therefore fewer places where
something can go wrong.

One entry point for search engines

If SEO is a thing you worry about, having a single site and set of URLs
is easier to manage.

Support for future and unknown devices

By design, RWD ignores specific devices and OSes, so a properly crafted RWD site automatically provides support for current and
future devices.

Downsides of RWD

There are some downsides to RWD. They might not be as readily apparent as the benefits, but they can have a detrimental effect on your
site's effectiveness.

Performance

Frontend performance on responsive sites can be a problem. For an
example that I'm guilty of myself, loading 5-10 full articles on the home
page of a blog might be OK on a fast broadband connection, but it's a
waste of bytes on a mobile network. Add in the typical desktop payload
of JavaScript, CSS, and images (which has doubled on average since
2010 (*http://bit.ly/uw-web-page-size*), by the way) and performance
can blow up in a big way. All the HTML, all of those images, all that
JavaScript, and all that CSS will be downloaded on all platforms,
whether they need it or not. Beyond content that might not be seen
because it's 50 screens down the page on a mobile device, you might
have certain functionality for the desktop version of your site, an image
carousel or tiled gallery, for example, that might be broken down to a
stacked series of images with no interactions on a phone. But yet,
you're still serving all that JavaScript code that has no real benefit for
a phone user.

Limited application flexibility

It's possible to build an application that is both usable and responsive, but it's also important to recognize that your users might have different needs on a phone versus their needs on a larger device. From my experience with financial services applications, the biggest need on mobile is to be able to view and interact with high-impact, focused events —either to respond to a problem with a specific transaction or to learn about some market event. On the desktop, the need is likely much more broad, offering access to an entire system, which in turn might be linked to other complicated systems. In financial services, the amount of information present on a single screen of a complicated application is overkill for a small screen. And that ignores the overall system complexity where a trader might be set up with three wide-screen monitors plastered with data from multiple sources. You can't interact with any of that data in any meaningful way on mobile unless it's broken down into smaller, digestible chunks. Trying to shoehorn both of those needs into the same codebase and relying on media queries alone, or media queries and some JavaScript to sort it, isn't going to serve your users well. This is especially true when you factor in the question of performance (a recurring theme with RWD).

Benefits of a Dedicated Mobile Experience

A dedicated mobile experience might not be the trendiest solution in web design circles right now, but providing a dedicated mobile experience has some serious benefits.

Performance optimized for specific devices

You can serve *just* the code you need for your mobile solution. That allows you to be as spare as you can be with the code that goes down the wire. The one exception to this is the demand, in the *m.example.com* pattern at least, to put in a redirect on the home page, which is going to cause a performance hit. That said, unless there's a hamster driving the server you're working on, these redirects are going to be measured in tens of milliseconds, which is still going to be faster than the download and parsing time of some of the images and JavaScript that would be needed for the desktop and ignored on mobile.

Heightened application flexibility

You've got a clean slate, so you can design a solution that works for your mobile-specific requirements without worrying about bytes (in the form of CSS, content, or images) that might be hitching a ride solely for the desktop.

Downsides of a Dedicated Mobile Experience

A dedicated mobile experience brings its own list of issues.

More complexity on the server side

With a dedicated mobile experience or even with a hybrid solution like RESS, once you step away from a pure RWD solution, you're going to be adding complexity on the server side in the form of redirects, DNS, and site setup or server-side scripting code (in PHP, C#, Ruby, Python, etc.).

Tougher maintenance

Unless you've got a large organization with separate teams for desktop and mobile views, you're going to have to manage more than one frontend codebase. If you've got a single pool of developers to maintain both codebases, it's simply harder to make sure they can all move between the two codebases efficiently. You can mitigate this with solid code standards and development best practices, but it's still something you have to manage.

Not as good for search engines

With multiple URLs, you've increased the complexity of your relationship with search engines. As you'll see in the section on redirects, you can manage it; you just need to know that you need to do it and how to do it.

Link management

If there's one thing I hate, it's clicking on an article link on Twitter on my phone and getting redirected to the mobile front page of the target site. Don't do that. If you do separate solutions, you need to make sure the bridge between the two is seamless. More on this later in the chapter.

You can miss detection of new and unknown devices

With the growing number of companies creating solid-to-great smartphones, there's a real danger in missing out, for at least some time, on the opportunity to serve your best content to a new device that can readily handle it.

Detection schemes that use the user agent string can be spoofed

At the end of the day, the user agent string is a malleable property of the browser. Users and browser vendors can both monkey with the user agent string in ways that you might not be prepared for if you're serving specific code for specific browsers and devices.

The User Agent String Can and Will Be Spoofed

There's a long history of user agent strings being spoofed in order to fool detection schemes. Because of the early popularity of Netscape Navigator and browser sniffing that blocked really terrible versions of Internet Explorer, almost every browser (Opera being an exception) identifies itself as "Mozilla." For a modern example, the Android browser, in addition to identifying itself as "Android," also identifies itself as both "Safari" and "Chrome."

That's the generic take on this technology spectrum. Let's take a quick look at some specifics.

If Facebook Jumped Off a Bridge, Would You Jump Off a Bridge, Too? Or: What Do the Biggest Sites in the United States Do?

So now that you know the fundamentals, let's take a look at an interesting data set. For a slightly different perspective, Table 4-1 lists the top 10 sites in the United States, according to Alexa. (*http://bit.ly/uw-alexa-top-us*) I hit each of those with a Samsung Galaxy Note II or a Chrome with a spoofed iPhone 4 user agent string, typing in the main site URL and then recording the results. I wanted to see what sites with practically unlimited budgets do to solve these issues. The takeaway from this little experiment was that the largest sites on the Internet uniformly redirect to a mobile-optimized subdomain or serve a fully mobile-optimized site. The one slight exception was Wikipedia, which serves a single global gateway page, only to redirect to a mobile-optimized subdomain for article pages.

This survey, therefore, shows clear results that go against the trend you might expect if you follow the web development sites, blogs, and Twitter accounts where RWD remains a hot topic.

Table 4-1. How the Alexa Top 10 Handles a Mobile Device

Original domain	Final domain	Result
google.com	google.com	At first glance, it might appear to be the same site. It's not. The downloaded source of the site generated when using a desktop device was 117KB on 2014-1-4. With a spoofed iPhone 4 user agent string, it was 10KB.
facebook.com	m.facebook.com	Mobile-optimized site
youtube.com	m.youtube.com	Mobile-optimized site
yahoo.com	m.yahoo.com	Mobile-optimized site
amazon.com	amazon.com	Mobile-optimized site. Same top-level domain (TLD), but a different path and markup than the desktop view.
ebay.com	m.ebay.com	Mobile-optimized site
wikipedia.org	wikipedia.org	Identical to desktop. Article pages are mobile-optimized, (e.g., *http://en.m.wikipedia.org/wiki/ Responsive_web_design*).
linkedin.com	touch.www.linkedin.com	Mobile-optimized site
twitter.com	mobile.twitter.com	Mobile-optimized site
bing.com	www.bing.com	Mobile-optimized site. Same TLD, same path, but different source. Oddly, on January 4, 2014, the spoofed iPhone 4 user agent string generated a slightly larger HTML file (44KB versus 48KB)

So, although none of these sites are infallible, it's instructive to see that people who can do *anything* are almost all choosing to do a dedicated mobile site. This doesn't mean that you should do the same simply because that's what the Facebooks of the world are doing, but it's what they do, and we can learn from their decisions.

For a slightly different perspective, Table 4-2 shows the top 10 sites in the Alexa news category (*http://bit.ly/uw-alexa-top-news*) and how they handle a mobile device. There are more RWD techniques here, but it's interesting (and also slightly confusing) to note that the best responsive site (from the BBC) performs a server redirect before serving a responsive site.

Even where the fit seems to be better, then, people with larger budgets are opting to do a dedicated mobile experience. There *are* two excellent examples of RWD here, one of which, *The Guardian*, is apparently going all in with RWD.

Table 4-2. How the Alexa top 10 news sites handle a mobile device

Original domain	Final domain	Result
news.yahoo.com	news.yahoo.com	Mobile-optimized site with RWD techniques. Shows different content based on the user agent. Different source. Desktop is 294KB. Mobile is 189KB.
huffingtonpost.com	m.huffpost.com/us/	Mobile-optimized site.
cnn.com	www.cnn.com	Mobile-optimized site.
reddit.com	reddit.com	Identical to desktop. The Reddit home page is somehwat fluid, so it "works" in different sizes. It breaks with very small screens. i.reddit.com exists, but isn't automatically redirected.
bbc.co.uk/news	m.bbc.co.uk/news	Redirects to an excellent responsive site.
weather.com/	m.weather.com/	A slick mobile web app.
nytimes.com	mobile.nytimes.com	As of January 19, 2014, this is a mobile-optimized site, even though the *Times* just released a redesign (*http://bit.ly/uw-nyt-redesign*).
news.google.com	news.google.com	Mobile-optimized site.
theguardian.com	theguardian.com	As of January 4, 2014, a responsive site which states proudly: "You're viewing an alpha release of the Guardian's responsive website."
forbes.com	forbes.com	Mobile-optimized site.

Beyond this look at the very top, there was recently a survey that indicated that up to 1/8 of the top 10,000 sites were responsive (*http://bit.ly/uw-responsive-sites*). This list included sites like starbucks.com (*http://www.starbucks.com/*), harvard.edu (*http://harvard.edu/*), time.com (*http://www.time.com/time/*), and worldwildlife.org (*http://worldwildlife.org/*). So, although the sites at the very top are going for a mobile-optimized solution, there *are* some very large, important sites going for the full RWD solutions.

Choose the Architecture That Makes Sense for Your Project

If there's not a one-size-fits-all approach to this, then what are you supposed to do? How do you choose which direction to go? This section lists some common guidelines for making this decision. This is a spectrum, so think of these rough guidelines as notable points on the wavelength of the responsive versus mobile site spectrum. There's not just blue and green. Teal is in there somewhere. Your solution might be the teal of web development.

Frontend developers and small teams

If you're doing a content site or simple application and are a frontend developer on a small team or are a team of one and are more focused on frontend technologies, then you want to go with RWD. Properly implemented, a responsive site can provide a great experience for a vast number of users, and the entire experience can be controlled on the frontend.

Content sites

If you're serving mostly text and image content, look to RWD, no matter what your skill set or team size. You can look to augment RWD with server-side solutions (particularly related to images and other media), but the techniques for responsive design are well established for this kind of content, so there's no reason not to go in that direction. If you pay careful attention to image sizes and limit the JavaScript payload, in order to keep things speedy, you can provide a great content experience across devices.

Applications

If you're building anything but the most basic application, look to doing a dedicated mobile experience. Form entry, visualizations, and interaction patterns might all benefit from optimization for large and small screens. You *may* be able to do a fully RWD application, but don't force the technique into your application if it doesn't make sense for your end users.

Big teams and big budgets

If you've got a large, skilled team, look for every opportunity to leverage the server. Whether that's with a dedicated mobile experience, or a responsive site aided and abetted by the server, there are going to be many opportunities to pass work back to the server and save your users bytes, connections, and processing time in the browser. Personally, this is where I'm happiest. Yes, I'm a frontend engineer, but I've been very fortunate over the years to work with some excellent engineers working on the server side. I can't count the number of times I've outlined a problem we typically have on the frontend, begun to talk through the potentially crazy lone-wolf approach ("Well, we could use JavaScript to…"), and been stopped by a super-smart backend engineer telling me, "No way dude, we can handle that edge-case and just serve you the good stuff." *I love that conversation.* I don't need to be the smartest guy in the room or do the most on the frontend just to prove that I can, so when someone comes up with a better solution that takes some of the heavy lifting off the client, I applaud that and get out of the way.

This is also what the biggest sites on the Web are doing, so you don't have to take my word for it.

Again, this is a spectrum, so there's no reason to do strictly one thing or the other. You need to take the options available to you, weigh them against the site or application you're building, and make your decision based on that. As with anything that people are passionate about, people can get a little tribal when it comes to the polar ends of this discussion. Don't fall in love with any solution, and you'll be better for it. If you want to have a fully responsive solution but still use your CDN's content negotiation to provide images optimized for the individual user agent, then go ahead and do that. You don't win points for architectural purity. You win points with fast, effective sites that work in a wide range of devices. You want the best balance between compatibility, design, and functionality.

All that being said, I will urge you to always err on the side of your users when weighing the benefits of all of these approaches. You can't always do the best thing for your users. I know this. I'm guilty of going for the easy solution on more than one occasion in order to just get something out the door. I'm also guilty of falling in love with development patterns without fully thinking through the effect on end users (or willfully ignoring it for convenience). With the goal of broad compatibility in mind, however, you need to guard against both of those impulses.

The rest of the chapter will look at some specific technical details and best practices related to redirects, device detection, responsive breakpoints, and server-side feature and capability detection. In addition to what's found here, there are also responsive and mobile components covered in Chapters 5, 6, and 7.

Redirects Should Resolve Logically

If you have a dedicated mobile experience that mirrors one-to-one the content on your desktop site, and you automatically redirect based on browser characteristics, then you should ensure that the page the user redirects to contains the expected content. If you redirect the user to your mobile home page, you've completely failed.

If for some reason the content doesn't exist in mobile form, don't redirect. Serve them the expected content.

It's hard to get people to click on links to your site. There are entire industries built around the art of getting people to follow links and read articles. ("Your Friend Clicked on a Link on Facebook, You'll Never Believe What Happened Next.") Celebrate the fact that the users are interested in what you're doing. Don't punish them for doing it on their phones.

The easiest way to deal with this is to just ensure that the path and associated content are identical on both the desktop domain and the mobile domain. For an example of this that's clear to see, look at Table 4-3 to see the way Twitter handles URLs. This is a perfectly clean solution. They simple insert "mobile" as a subdomain, and everything else maps one-to-one.

Table 4-3. Twitter's mobile and desktop URLs

Page	Desktop URL	Mobile URL
Connect	*https://twitter.com/i/connect*	*https://mobile.twitter.com/i/connect*
Profile	*https://twitter.com/robreact*	*https://mobile.twitter.com/robreact*
Tweet	*https://twitter.com/robreact/status/ 412431960791719936*	*https://mobile.twitter.com/robreact/status/ 412431960791719936*

Huffington Post also handles this well, although they handle it in a slightly different way (Table 4-4). On the desktop, the URLs contain search engine friendly keywords based on the title of the article and the article ID, a seven-digit string. On mobile, the URL only contains the seven digit article ID, creating a slightly shorter URL, which is both fewer bytes and easier to type on a mobile device.

Table 4-4. Huffington Post's mobile and desktop URLs

Article	Desktop URL	Mobile URL
Pope Francis Leaves Nuns A Voicemail That You Have To Hear	*http://www.huffingtonpost.com/ 2014/01/03/pope-francis-nuns-voicemail_n_4536709.html*	*http://m.huffpost.com/us/entry/ 4536709*
Banksy Graffiti Gets Vandalized In Sundance Town	*http://www.huffingtonpost.com/ 2014/01/03/banksy-vandalized_n_4537545.html*	*http://m.huffpost.com/us/entry/ 4537545*
Weird Amazon *Web* Structures Built By Spiders, Scientists Discover (VIDEO)	*http://www.huffingtonpost.com/ 2014/01/06/amazon-web-structures-spiders_n_4548547.html*	*https://mobile.twitter.com/ robreact/status/ 412431960791719936*

They can get away with this duplicate content (two separate URLs serving the exact same content) on the search engine front by using a canonical link relation (*http://bit.ly/uw-canonical-urls*). Canonical links define a preferred URL for similar content, so it's good to define one on your mobile site in order to ensure that the Googles and Bings of the world are looking at the correct page for search engine ranking.

Show 'Em What You Got

If, for some reason, you can't serve mobile-optimized content, then serve the desktop content. Your users clicked on a link expecting some sort of payoff. It might be a bummer to serve them a full desktop experience, but it's *much* worse to confuse and frustrate them with a balmy redirect.

The canonical relation is straightforward syntax-wise. As the following snippet pulled from my blog shows, it's just the relation attribute with a property of "canonical" and then the URL of the resources that should be treated as the resource of record:

```
<link rel="canonical"
href="http://htmlcssjavascript.com/web/it-well-do-it-live/">
```

How to accomplish the redirect itself is a two-part effort. First, you need to understand how to do the redirect, and then you need to serve different content. I won't try to show you how to serve separate templates because there are many platforms and technologies you could be using and a lesson for one might not be at all useful for another. I will, however, talk about how to do the redirect.

Redirect Options

As I mentioned, there are a few different ways you can do this redirect: a simple redirect (mobile or not mobile), or one based on device characteristics using a web service or Device Description Repository (DDR).

Simple Redirection

The basic pattern for a simple redirect is illustrated in the following code samples. In these, you'll do a simple redirect based on the user agent string. It's a simple redirect, in that it's either a mobile user agent or it's not, and it redirects (or doesn't) accordingly. The regular expression is from detectmobilebrowsers.com (*http://detectmobile browsers.com/*), an open source project that parses major (and not so major) mobile user agent strings to create a pretty comprehensive regular expression to detect a mobile device. There are versions for pretty much every programming language. This example is in JavaScript, which is as close to a lingua franca as the Web has today, but the logic will be the same, no matter what language you're using on the server side.

There are two things happening. First, you set a click event handler to manually move the user over to the mobile site. It uses `window.ses sionStorage` to set a flag indicating the user's choice of the mobile site. Following that is the redirect code. It starts with an `if...else` block, which is where our tests are executed. The first case tests against the `sessionStorage` variable to quickly short circuit further logic if there's a match. If there's no match, we go into an `else` block where there are two variables, `primaryMobileRegex` and `secondaryMobileRegex`, which represent two different regular expressions. The first regular expression tests for the most obvious and most popular mobile devices in the hope that these likelier use cases will resolve `true` without having to evaluate the much larger secondary test. The second, larger test offers broader coverage, but only if the first test fails. If there's no value in `sessionStorage`, then you test against the regular expressions, redirecting to the mobile option that either of them are matching.

Also, notice the link element with the "alternate" `rel` attribute and associated media query. This is a hint indicating the presence of mobile-optimized content. Coupling this pattern with a rel="canonical" link element is the full pattern preferred by Google when creating an alternate mobile experience:

```html
<!DOCTYPE html>
<html class="no-js">
  <head>
    <title>Mobile Detection</title>
    <link rel="alternate"
      media="only screen and (max-width: 640px)"
      href="ch04-02-mobile.html" >
  </head>
  <body>
    <h1>Desktop!</h1>
    <p><a href="ch04-02-mobile.html"
         id="switch">Go to the mobile version</a>
    </p>
    <script>
      document.getElementById( "switch" ).addEventListener(
      "click" ,
      function(){
        sessionStorage.setItem( "view" , "mobile" );
        window.location = this.href;
      });
      (function( UAString,url ){
        if ( sessionStorage.getItem( "view" ) == "desktop") {
          return
        } else if ( sessionStorage.getItem( "view" )
                  == "mobile" ) {
          window.location=url;
        } else {
        var primaryMobileRegex = /(android|bb\d+|meego).
          +mobile|avantgo|bada\/
          |blackberry|blazer|compal|elaine|fennec|hiptop|
          iemobile|ip(hone|od)|iris|kindle|lge |maemo|midp|
          mmp|mobile.+firefox|netfront|opera m(ob|in)i|palm( os)
          ?|phone|p(ixi|re)\/|plucker|pocket|psp|series(4|6)0|
          symbian|treo|up\.(browser|link)|vodafone|wap|windows
          (ce|phone)|xda|xiino/i;
        var secondaryMobileRegex = /1207|6310|6590|3gso|4thp|
          50[1-6]i|770s|802s|a wa|abac|ac(er|oo|s\-)|ai(ko|rn)|
          al(av|ca|co)|amoi|an(ex|ny|yw)|aptu|ar(ch|go)|as(te
          |us)|attw|au(di|\-m|r |s )|avan|be(ck|ll|nq)|bi(lb|rd)
          |bl(ac|az)|br(e|v)w|bumb|bw\-(n|u)|c55\/|capi|ccwa|cdm
          \-|cell|chtm|cldc|cmd\-|co(mp|nd)|craw|da(it|ll|ng)
          |dbte|dc\-s|devi|dica|dmob|do(c|p)o|ds(12|\-d)|el(49
          |ai)|em(l2|ul)|er(ic|k0)|esl8|ez([4-7]0|os|wa|ze)|fetc
          |fly(\-|_)|g1 u|g560|gene|gf\-5|g\-mo|go(\.w|od)|gr(ad
          |un)|haie|hcit|hd\-(m|p|t)|hei\-|hi(pt|ta)|hp(i|ip)|hs
          \-c|ht(c(\-| |_|a|g|p|s|t)|tp)|hu(aw|tc)|i\-(20|go|ma)
          |i230|iac( |\-|\/)|ibro|idea|ig01|ikom|im1k|inno|ipaq|
          iris|ja(t|v)a|jbro|jemu|jigs|kddi|keji|kgt( |\/)|klon|
```

```
kpt |kwc\-|kyo(c|k)|le(no|xi)|lg( g|\/(k|l|u)|50|54|\-
[a-w])|libw|lynx|m1\-w|m3ga|m50\/|ma(te|ui|xo)|mc(01
|21|ca)|m\-cr|me(rc|ri)|mi(o8|oa|ts)|mmef|mo(01|02|bi|
de|do|t(\-| |o|v)|zz)|mt(50|p1|v )|mwbp|mywa|n10[0-2]|
n20[2-3]|n30(0|2)|n50(0|2|5)|n7(0(0|1)|10)|ne((c|m)\-|
on|tf|wf|wg|wt)|nok(6|i)|nzph|o2im|op(ti|wv)|oran|owg1
|p800|pan(a|d|t)|pdxg|pg(13|\-([1-8]|c))|phil|pire|pl
(ay|uc)|pn\-2|po(ck|rt|se)|prox|psio|pt\-g|qa\-a|qc(07
|12|21|32|60|\-[2-7]|i\-)|qtek|r380|r600|raks|rim9|ro
(ve|zo)|s55\/|sa(ge|ma|mm|ms|ny|va)|sc(01|h\-|oo|p\-)
|sdk\/|se(c(\-|0|1)|47|mc|nd|ri)|sgh\-|shar|sie(\-|m)
|sk\-0|sl(45|id)|sm(al|ar|b3|it|t5)|so(ft|ny)|sp(01|h
\-|v\-|v )|sy(01|mb)|t2(18|50)|t6(00|10|18)|ta(gt|lk)
|tcl\-|tdg\-|tel(i|m)|tim\-|t\-mo|to(pl|sh)|ts(70|m\-
|m3|m5)|tx\-9|up(\.b|g1|si)|utst|v400|v750|veri|vi(rg
|te)|vk(40|5[0-3]|\-v)|vm40|voda|vulc|vx(52|53|60|61
|70|80|81|83|85|98)|w3c(\-| )|webc|whit|wi(g |nc|nw)
|wmlb|wonu|x700|yas\-|your|zeto|zte\
-/i;
if( primaryMobileRegex.test( UAString ) ||
  secondaryMobileRegex.test( UAString.substr( 0,4 ))){
      window.location=url;
  }
 }
})( navigator.userAgent ||
  navigator.vendor ||
  window.opera,'ch04-02-mobile.html' );
</script>
</body>
</html>
```

In case you're curious, the argument to the detection function is built up by testing three possible variations on the user agent string or equivalent. `navigator.userAgent` is by far the most common. So common, in fact, I don't even know the specific situations where `navigator.userAgent` would fail and fall back to `navigator.vendor` or the Opera specific `window.opera`. All I know is they're there for whatever arcane situations demand them, and that's good enough for me.

The mobile landing page is simpler. All it has is a click event handler set on the link to return to the desktop experience, setting a "desktop" flag with `sessionStorage.setItem`:

```
<!DOCTYPE html>
<html class="no-js">
  <head>
    <title>Mobile Landing Device</title>
    <link rel="canonical" href="ch04-02.html" >
  </head>
  <body>
```

```
<h1>You've Got a Mobile Device</h1>
<p><a href="ch04-02.html"
     id="switch">Go to the desktop version</a>
</p>
<script>
  document.getElementById( "switch" )
    .addEventListener( "click" ,
      function(){
        sessionStorage.setItem( "view" , "desktop" );
        window.location = this.href;
    });
</script>
</body>
</html>
```

Web Storage

If you're not familiar with the web storage specification and want to use it, keep in mind that sessionStorage only lasts for the current session. If you want to save user preference for a longer time in the browser, you can use localStorage, which is for longer-term storage. It has the same API as sessionStorage. It just lasts longer.

If you're using these, you should take a look at the web storage polyfills (*http://bit.ly/uw-web-storage-polyfills*) on the Modernizr site.

You could alternatively just use cookies for this. This would be especially helpful if you're doing a server-side redirect because the server would have the same access to cookies that the browser would. I prefer the web storage interface, but the ability to share state easily across the browser and server is valuable.

Options for More Complicated Queries

If you want to do more complicated queries based on deeper device characteristics, there are a few options, none of which are perfect. There are some cloud-based solutions like DeviceAtlas (*https://deviceatlas.com/*) that are going to be easier to implement, but come at a cost. On the other end, there's the OpenDDR project, which is free and open source, but isn't nearly as easy to use as a cloud-based solution (especially if you're not using C# or Java, the two sample implementations that ship with the project).

That said, if you've got the money for a paid service, or the time and the patience for the OpenDDR project, they are useful because they

---

allow you to query for device characteristics (much in the way media queries work) and not just query against the user agent string. A sample of the data available in the OpenDDR can be seen in the following XML snippet. It shows the information recorded on the Samsung Galaxy S4. As you can see, it gives information about both the physical characteristics (screen size, touchscreen), software (browser and OS) and browser capabilities, including core JavaScript capabilities and the ability to inline images (a common performance technique):

```xml
<device id="SPH-L720" parentId="genericSamsung">
  <property name="model" value="SPH-L720"/>
  <property name="marketing_name" value="Galaxy S4"/>
  <property name="displayWidth" value="1080"/>
  <property name="displayHeight" value="1920"/>
  <property name="mobile_browser" value="Android WebKit"/>
  <property name="mobile_browser_version" value="4.0"/>
  <property name="device_os" value="Android"/>
  <property name="device_os_version" value="4.2.2"/>
  <property name="inputDevices" value="touchscreen"/>
  <property name="dual_orientation" value="true"/>
  <property name="ajax_support_javascript" value="true"/>
  <property name="ajax_support_getelementbyid" value="true"/>
  <property name="ajax_support_inner_html" value="true"/>
  <property name="ajax_manipulate_dom" value="true"/>
  <property name="ajax_manipulate_css" value="true"/>
  <property name="ajax_support_events" value="true"/>
  <property name="ajax_support_event_listener" value="true"/>
  <property name="image_inlining" value="true"/>
  <property name="from" value="oddr"/>
</device>
```

For my money (or, more often, my client's money), I think the simple redirect is going to be good enough when coupled with responsive techniques—with one exception. Getting access to the device pixels per inch from services like DeviceAtlas (*http://bit.ly/uw-deviceatlas-data*) when working with an image-heavy site, and the task of being able to properly load images to match the device capabilities would be useful. There are browser-based solutions to this issue, which you'll learn about in Chapter 6, but this is great information to have.

Always Offer an Escape from the Mobile Version

As I previously described, I hate being on a mobile device and being redirected to the mobile home page of the site instead of content specified in the navigated link. One way that this can be somewhat mitigated is by offering easy access to the full site via a link or button on the home page. If I can get to the desktop site, I can usually find the content one way or another (browse or search, if it's not content directly on the home page). If I'm redirected to the home page, and there's no easy way to request the desktop site, then that's just about the worst thing possible.

The Trifecta of Mobile User Antagonism

Actually, redirecting to the home page, *adding an interstitial imploring me to download an Android or iOS app when I get there*, and not offering a link to the desktop site would be the worst thing possible.

Alternatively, if you have an application with a dedicated mobile experience that handles the most common use cases, keep in mind the occasional emergency where someone on his phone might need to access a feature only available on the desktop, even if it means working through a desktop interface with fat fingers.

So, if you have a dedicated mobile experience, you need to offer a way to cross over to the desktop version. You've already seen this in action in the previous section. But from a design perspective, a simple link, like this one provided by the BBC (Figure 4-4) is probably sufficient. Just make sure it's clearly labeled.

Make It Count

Even though you've already seen this in the previous example, it's worth stressing—you *must* ensure that, once a user crosses over to the desktop site, you keep her on the desktop site. Whatever redirection scheme you use must be able to be overridden by the user's actions for the length of her session. If she chooses the desktop site, don't randomly redirect her back to the mobile site halfway through her site journey.

Additionally, offer the ability to move back to the mobile site via an equivalent link. Especially in the case of an application with different feature sets on mobile and desktop, the ability to cross back and forth is vital.

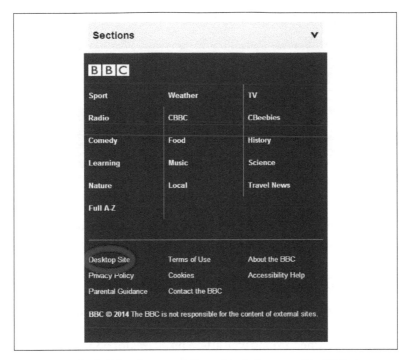

Figure 4-4. Switching from mobile to the desktop on the BBC site

An excellent example of how to handle this hybrid approach, providing an optimized mobile experience where possible and seamlessly falling back to the desktop experience where it's not, can be seen with the mobile site from Heritage Auctions, "the world's third largest auctioneer" (Figure 4-5). The majority of the common tasks, such as searching for and browsing auction items, are served through a dedicated mobile interface. Less common tasks (in this case, working with their want list feature) are passed back to the desktop display.

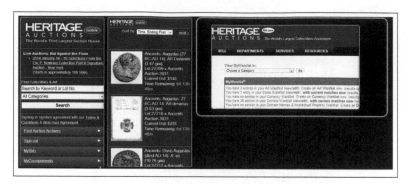

Figure 4-5. Creating a want list with Heritage Auctions

It might not be perfect, as in this case where landscape mode was required, but you're always assured of getting the task done.

Be Fluid and Design for Your Design

If you look at many responsive sites, you will see breakpoints set to "standard" measurements (320px, 480px, 768px, 1024px, 1280px). These are all defined around typical CSS pixel sizes for popular devices: iPhones (portrait and landscape), iPads (portrait and landscape), and large-screen desktops. This is OK, but you could potentially save yourself some time and proof yourself against unknown devices by making decisions based on the requirements of your particular site. You can let the design itself dictate the breakpoints. For a simplified example, if you're publishing a typical blog with two columns (one large for articles and one smaller for ads and sidebar links), and you have fluid grids that take up a percentage of the screen, then you may have just one major breakpoint for the entire site. This might be the point where the sidebar disappears altogether or floats below the main content. Although that breakpoint *might* be the width of an iPad in portrait mode (768 pixels), it might not be. With this concept, coupled with the use of relative units and the max-width and min-width CSS properties to keep things from going crazy, you should be all set with the majority of screen sizes, known and unknown.

This simplified example shows a sketch of how this might look. The HTML is straightforward. Although it uses all HTML5 sectioning elements (<header>, <main>, article, <aside>, and <footer>) and assigns WAI-ARIA roles to them, if you swapped out the tag names for ids (`<div id="header">`), then this markup would look like a typical blog layout from 10 years ago:

```html
<!DOCTYPE html>
<html class="no-js">
  <head>
    <meta charset="utf-8">
    <meta name="viewport" content="width=device-width,
        initial-scale=1">
    <link href="responsive.css" rel="stylesheet"
      type="text/css">
    <script
      src="../_assets/js/vendor/modernizr-2.6.3.min.js">
    </script>
  </head>
  <body>
    <div class="container">
      <header role="banner">
        <h1>Responsive Header!</h1>
      </header>
      <main id="content" class="group" role="main">
        <article>
          <h1>Syndication</h1>
          <p>Eu actually fugiat flexitarian Odd Future single
          origin coffee. Next level ugh actually pour-over,
          farm-to-table artisan McSweeney's magna polaroid tofu.
          Locavore dreamcatcher Shoreditch skateboard. Tumblr
          placeat commodo, Marfa DIY typewriter master cleanse
          tote bag food truck Neutra Austin mumblecore
          accusamus. Est ennui drinking vinegar
          </p>
        </article>
        <aside>
          <a href="http://hipsteripsum.me/">Text generated with
          Hipster Ipsum. Which is so old it's now ironic.</a>
        </aside>
      </main>
      <footer role="contentinfo"><small>How are you?</small>
      </footer>
    </div>
  </body>
</html>
```

The CSS is where the magic happens. In this example, the containing div is set to 100% of the body, with a max-width of 75ems, which maps to 1200px at a default font size of 16px. There's more on the use of ems in the next section, On Relative Units. The main element is set to use the new flexbox ("flexible box") display mode with its corresponding flex-direction property set to row. This combination ensures that the article and aside will fit side by side in a row, with each filling the available space. In practice, you would add this test to your Modernizr build and use the Modernizr.flexbox Boolean or the .flexbox class on the html element to provide fallbacks for browsers that don't yet support flexbox. Here I'm just assuming you've got a newer web browser in order to run this demo.

The header element has a background image set to have a background-size of 100%. This ensures that the background will scale as the page size increases or decreases.

Following that, there's a single media query set at 40em (640px at the standard default font size) that changes the flex-direction property to column, which pushes the article and aside elements into a single column, better suited to smaller screens. It also swaps out the large header image for one that works better at smaller resolutions:

```
@charset "utf-8";
.container {
  margin: auto;
  width: 100%;
  max-width: 80em;
}
main {
  display: flex;
  flex-direction: row;
}
article {
  border: 1px solid #06C;
  width: 70%;
  padding: 1em;
}
aside {
  border: 1px solid #060;
  width: 30%;
  padding: 1em;
}
header h1 {
  line-height: 2em;
  margin: 0;
  text-shadow: 1px 1px 3px #888;
}
header {
  padding: .2em 1em;
  background-image: url(responsive-header.jpg);
  background-size: 100%;
  background-repeat: no-repeat;
  background-color: #2492b4;
  height: 32.1875em;
```

```
    color: #fff;
    background-position: top;
}

/*
Major breakpoint
*/
@media all and (max-width: 40em) {
  main {
    flex-direction: column;
  }
  article {
    width: 100%;
  }
  aside {
    width: 100%;
  }
  header {
    border: 1px solid #000;
    text-align: center;
    background-color: #0d9c2b;
  }
}
```

Although you could stop there and have a perfectly usable site, you can add some small touches to the CSS that will improve the layout across the device spectrum without too much effort. To do that, you can tweak the design of the header element using minor breakpoints.

Feel Free to Abuse Minor Breakpoints

The following CSS sample shows how this can be accomplished. For starters, in the first four zones, you'll adjust the height of the header to better match the shrinking width of the header image better. At the smaller sizes, the background image itself is swapped out for one more suited to a vertical layout.

With all of these, I started with standard dimensions, but tweaked as necessary, depending on the way it looked. So although you will see certain em measurements that match common dimensions, there are others that are chosen simply because the design needed a tweak at that level. Based on a default 16-pixel font size, 46 ems equals 736 pixels, and 32 ems equals 512 pixels:

```
/*
Minor breakpoints
*/
@media all and (min-width: 64em) and (max-width: 72em) {
```

```
    header {
      height: 30em;
    }
  }

  @media all and (min-width: 46em) and (max-width: 64em) {
    header {
      height: 24em;
    }
  }

  @media all and (min-width: 40em) and (max-width: 46em) {
    header {
      height: 18em;
    }
  }

  @media all and (min-width: 32em) and (max-width: 40em) {
    header {
      background-image: url(responsive-header-thin.jpg);
      height: 42em;
      background-position: center;
      padding: .1em .5em;
    }
  }

  @media all and (max-width: 32em) {
    header {
      background-image: url(responsive-header-super-thin.jpg);
      height: 24em;
      background-size: auto;
      padding: .1em .2em;
      background-position: bottom;
    }
    header h1 {
      font-size: 1em;
    }
  }
```

Using Brad Frost's fun, if scary, tool ish (*http://bit.ly/uw-ish*), you can see that the layout flows and functions pretty well across a wide range of resolutions, not just popular device widths (Figure 4-6).

Figure 4-6. The output from Brad Frost's ish

This is a simplified example, but recognizing that you don't have to go all-in at popular device widths and instead can work within the confines of your design is important. Your design and the requirements of your site should be the driving factors of the breakpoints you choose.

On Relative Units

Relative units are your friends. ems, which you probably already know about, as well as rems, vhs, and vws are all going to help you create fluid solutions. If you're not familiar, here's a quick summary:

em

> An em is equivalent to the height of the current font. They were very popular for a brief period for all measurements on a page when the default "text increase" behavior in browsers was to simply increase the size of the text without adjusting the size of the boxes. This em-based measurement system was great as it made for layouts that would smoothly increase when the text was increased. There were certain difficulties in this approach because of the fact that the em measurement can change, depending on the size of the font in that section of the document, but they weren't insurmountable. When the default behavior changed to zooming the entire page, they fell out of favor once again, and pixels reigned supreme. The pendulum has begun to swing back toward ems, as they can bring some benefit in responsive designs. Setting breakpoints in ems, for example, allows a zoomed-in interface to react to breakpoints even when the underlying pixel measurements haven't changed (*http://bit.ly/uw-ems-rwd*).

rem

A rem is a "root em," the em value of the font defined on the root element. This brings all of the benefit of using ems without the complexity that changing font sizes can bring.

vh

A vh is equal to 1% of the viewport height.

vw

A vw is equal to 1% of the viewport width. These units allow for viewport relative layouts. If the viewport changes (say in the change from portrait to landscape on a tablet), these units will scale proportionally.

Because of the use of relative units, rems, the breakpoints in the previous example are triggered, even though the underlying screen size (in this case, 1600 pixels) never changes (Figure 4-7).

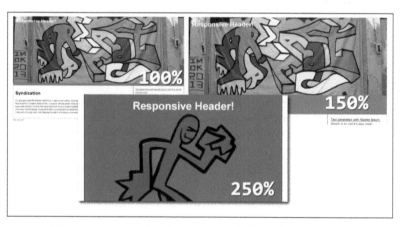

Figure 4-7. Showing breakpoints triggered when the page is zoomed

There's more to these techniques than is presented here, of course, and the implementation details will change based on your specific needs. That said, the idea of being as fluid as you can be with your layout, of letting the design dictate your breakpoints, and for using minor breakpoints to fine-tune your layout, if needed, are all going to serve you well going forward.

"Accepting the Ebb and Flow of Things"

With an open mind and a full toolbox of techniques, your options for managing the full device spectrum are about as limitless as the number of devices. By taking advantage of the server where possible and focusing on the needs of your application throughout the design process, you can provide a solid experience for everyone hitting your site, no matter what the size or shape of the device they're carrying.

CHAPTER 5

Working with User Input

No great genius has ever existed without some touch of madness.

— Seneca

Although I *am* the kind of guy that would write a book about broad compatibility and serving the broadest possible user base, I'm not usually the kind of user who unwittingly uncovers problems with developers applying hard-and-fast rules to a problem that requires a more nuanced approach. I've always got good hardware, and I run popular, up-to-date browsers. I should get the best experience possible whenever I get on the Web, and all but the most myopic developers are going to serve me something that will work.

This was *generally* the case until I got a touchscreen laptop. Once I brought home a Windows 8 laptop, things started to get a little weird. Pretty much every day I run into a site that has guessed wrong about my setup in one way or another. This ranges from the catastrophic to the minor, but there's always *something*. Watch me at a coffee shop and just wait for me to click something a couple of times with a mouse or touchpad, see nothing happen, smirk, and then touch the same element with a finger in order to activate it. This simple error, only listening for touch events, is very common and speaks to a fundamental misunderstanding of the nature of user input on the Web.

Hopefully, this chapter will make life better for me and everyone else out there with multiple input modes.

Not that the case of multiple input modes on the same device is the only issue on the Web today in regards to user input. Touchscreen laptops are only the latest front in this ongoing struggle to properly capture user input and react to it in a way that makes sense for both users and developers. The question of how to manage user input, be it by mouse, keyboard, pen, speech, or gesture, has always been tricky. This problem is made worse by the fact that developers have only recently begun to focus on the question in the correct way. Although it's still very common to see sites that use simplistic tests to switch between an interface that relies on traditional mouse events and one that relies on touch events, more and more talk (*http://bit.ly/uw-touchandmouse*) is now focused (*http://bit.ly/uw-gettingtouchy*) on how best to deal with multiple input modes without treating it like a binary choice.

This chapter will examine the various factors at play when working with user input on the modern Web. For starters, we'll look at the variety of devices and input modes out there that might be hitting your site. Additionally, we'll look at the logic trap that still has developers testing for "touch" devices and generating faulty results by using bum logic. In particular, we'll look at why the common "touch" detection schemes are flawed. Building off of that, we'll then look at some strategies for designing interfaces that work well across all input types. We'll then focus on the technical factors that you need to take into account to manage multiple input modes on the modern Web.

This is one area that is going to only get more confusing in the future, so if there's one aspect of modern development where embracing uncertainty will make your life easier, this is it. Forget about trying to guess what users are going to use to interact with your site. Simply be ready for them to interact, and get out of the way as best you can.

The State of User Input on the Web

Based on the conversations I see on GitHub and Twitter, the basic landscape isn't clear to people. Many developers and designers are iPhone/Mac-based, so they live in a binary world without many of the innovations in input mode that are increasingly common in the Windows and Android worlds. Because of that, let's look at the way that multiple input modes work in the real world (using myself as a test subject) and why approaching it with a focus on embracing uncertainty is going to be the healthiest way to go forward.

My personal gear is a treasure trove of input modes. Let's examine the device configurations I can potentially use in a day. As you look at this, keep in mind there are plenty of alternative configurations (think:

Chromebooks or any number of other convertible laptops) that can have similar flexibility. I'm just a handy example. You might not be able to walk a mile in my shoes, but a little empathy for me might help you make smarter decisions going forward.

If just one person asks, "Would this screw Rob up?" after reading this section, I've done my job well (Figure 5-1).

Figure 5-1. A selection of the author's devices and device configurations

In a typical week, I might use:

- A Windows 8.1 laptop set up as a workstation. The laptop is a touchscreen. The second monitor is not. I work on the large monitor so I'm generally confined to just a mouse and keyboard, even if I still have a touchscreen on one of my screens.

- A convertible laptop (a Lenovo Yoga to be precise) running Windows 8.1 and set up as a laptop. This is a traditional laptop that also has a touchscreen. It has a trackpad, and I occasionally run an external mouse on it.

- The Lenovo Yoga in tablet mode. In this configuration, the *only* input is touch. The trackpad, which is now folded to the back, is turned off.

- The Lenovo Yoga, in tablet mode, with a Wacom tablet attached. This is a fine-grained pointing device that works, effectively, like a mouse, even if the rest of the device is a tablet.

- The Lenovo Yoga, in laptop mode, with a Wacom tablet attached. This is basically *two* mice *and* a touchscreen.

- A Samsung Galaxy Note II. This is a typical, *if really big*, smartphone.

- The Galaxy Note II with the stylus out. This pen is as fine-grained as a mouse and offers hover capability. I often use this when I'm visiting a site that only has a desktop view.

Should I also point out that I will use a keyboard to navigate a site or application whenever possible? I think I should. The traditional methods for ensuring that keyboard users can access content and functionality still apply.

Keep in mind that all of these modes can change at any time. So even if you were able to recognize that I was running the Yoga in tablet mode at the opening of a browsing session, you couldn't know for sure that it would remain in that configuration for the remainder of the session. That's the point of having a device like that, after all, being able to switch contexts and features as needed. I will often go into "tent" mode when watching video, so any tabs that are open at that point would have their original assumptions squashed by my desire to put my laptop on my coffee table in order to sit on my couch and watch web video.

Let's take a minute to look at the traditional methods of detecting touch capability and why a positive result doesn't mean what many people think it means. There are two ways this detection falls apart—technical and conceptual. Let's look at the conceptual issue first.

The Conceptual Problem with "Touch" Detection

As my case illustrates, there's no simple divide between mouse users and touch users. Even if you're willing to throw away the false positives and negatives that any of the technical approaches to testing might bring, forking your code in an `if…else` based on one of the testing schemes that follows ignores the problem illustrated by my setup. Even if you can accurately detect users with touch *capabilities*, you can't know for certain that they will only ever need touch. Knowing what you now know about the spectrum of input modes, what can you safely do with that information? You can *enhance* an interface, but you can't wall one off based on mouse versus touch.

We'll look at some concrete examples of how this can break later in this chapter. Before we do, let's take a look at the basic technical problems with detecting touch.

The Technical Problem with "Touch" Detection

If you follow any open source project with any sort of popularity, you will eventually see nagging issues that come up repeatedly. These can be issues that are hard to solve, issues that are solved but not in a way that people might expect, issues that need better documentation, issues with controversial resolutions, or any number of other reasons. One such nagging issue on the Modernizr project is the purpose behind and meaning of the result of the `modernizr.touch` test.

Because of this, the Modernizr repo has been one of the central sources of research and discussion on the technical challenges of detecting a touchscreen. Lucky for us, Modernizr dev Stu Cox has written up a lot of his research about the question (*http://bit.ly/uw-cox*). Looking at his research and adding on to it, the fundamental issues are as follows.

Using touch APIs to detect "touch" is faulty

The most common test for "touch" is to search for `ontouchstart` in the `window` object. As you'll see in depth in the examples later in this chapter, it's an unreliable test if your goal is to separate out mouse users from users with touchscreens, because many users can be both. It's also unreliable if you're just trying to figure out if a user has raw touch capabilities.

For one thing, there's nothing stopping a browser vendor from implementing touch APIs or exposing the event handlers in the DOM. In fact, this is exactly what Chrome 24 did, shipping with these APIs always available no matter what the configuration or capabilities of the device were.

Additionally, browsers and OSes can conspire to throw out wonky results. If the OS reports that a touchscreen is available, because of a bug or some setting, then the browser will just have to report the false positive. This has been seen with both Firefox and Chrome on Windows 8 and some BlackBerry devices.

Modernizr.touch Is Dead

This has been such a problem for Modernizr that it's gone to the extreme length of renaming the test from `Modern izr.touch` to `Modernizr.touchevents` in order to better describe what the test is actually looking for—the presence of the touch event's API in the browser.

This test also fails because the Internet Explorer desktop browsers that recognize gestures implement a different (and in my mind, superior) model for inputs called *pointer events*. They get their own section in this chapter, but in short, it's an input event model that combines touch, mouse, pen, and anything else you can imagine into a unified pointer model. So, even though Internet Explorer 10 and 11 on the desktop have a great interface for gestures, the simplistic `ontouch start in window` test fails there.

Small screen might not be touch—large screen might be

The dawn of everyday touchscreen computing was with the iPhone. So, for at least a little while, if you were presented with a good browser (it supported media queries, for example) and it had a small screen, you could assume it was a smartphone and was therefore "touch." Conversely, every other good browser was probably a desktop device.

This was never a great idea (there are decent mobile browsers on devices without touchscreen), and nowadays with the full spectrum of devices with or without touchscreen capability, it's basically useless. A flip phone running Opera Mobile would have media queries and report it was a small screen, but not have touch capability, and a tablet or touch-capable laptop would have a mighty big screen but would possess touch capability.

The future isn't here yet

There are technologies that might help with this on the horizon. The pointer media query, for example, will allow you to test for "coarse" (think finger) or "fine" pointers (mouse, stylus), but this isn't widely implemented yet and even if it were, it still falls into the trap of obscuring the presence of a mouse or stylus on a device with touchscreen plus some other input. Testing at quirksmode.org (*http://bit.ly/uw-pointertest*) with the latest Chrome, this media query reports "coarse" for me, as Figure 5-2 shows.

I *can* touch my screen, sure. But as I've already pointed out, I can also have a mouse or pen attached to this machine, so reporting "coarse" for me doesn't tell the whole story. I'm also in possession of a fine-grained control.

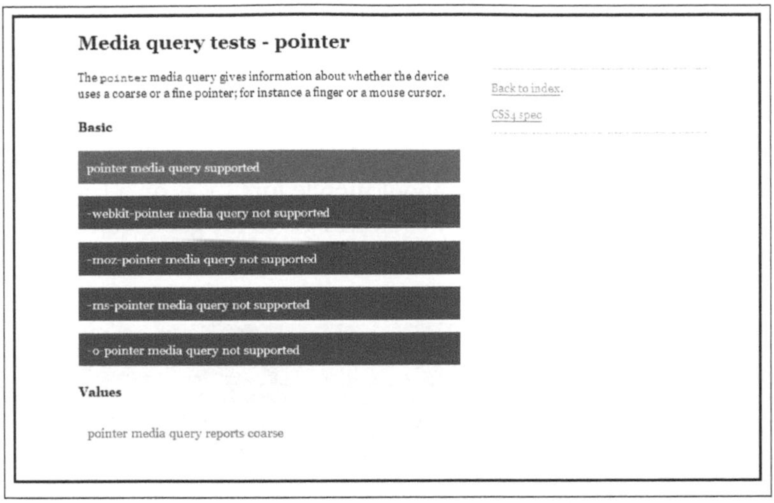

Figure 5-2. The result of the media query for "pointer"

Now that we've seen the troubles with trying to detect this stuff, let's look at how these issues can cause problems for your users.

What It Means to Get It Wrong

Because I'm writing these words on a laptop with a touchscreen, and I'm constantly (if unintentionally) trolled by developers messing up touch detection in one way or another, let me start this section with a couple of examples that I've captured over the past year of developers developing for a "yes touch" or "no touch" world.

This section will look at a couple of examples of how failing to get this right can have a detrimental effect on your users. These examples aren't from fly-by-night operations, either, so a significant number of people witnessed these examples in the wild. The first represents the danger of looking at this simplistically. With one faulty piece of logic, your site can simply fail to work in a browser that can easily support all the technologies under the hood. The second represents a small error in logic that degrades the user experience in a subtle, but annoying way.

You Can Fail Completely

In December of 2013, I was excited to learn that Spotify had launched a "year in review" mini-app full of visualizations of different personal and global trends in music. I love music, I'm a Spotify user (*http://*

open.spotify.com/user/robreact), and I love cool visualizations on the Web (*http://bit.ly/uw-data-viz*), so I was excited to check it out.

Except I couldn't.

I clicked through and was greeted with the message in Figure 5-3. I was confused. What do I care about mobile for? I was on a laptop. I wasn't on a mobile device. Why couldn't I get to the good stuff?

Figure 5-3. Spotify's year in review falsely reporting a Windows 8 laptop as a mobile device

I loaded Firefox and got the same result. I started to have a hint of what was wrong. Seizing on the hint, I loaded the site in Internet Explorer (Figure 5-4). It worked. My hunch was right. The Spotify team was using the `Modernizr.touch` test as a simple mobile/nonmobile gateway. The reason the site was viewable in IE was the fact that IE doesn't expose `ontouchstart` in the `window` object, and the presence of `window.ontouchstart` is the heart of the Modernizr test.

Figure 5-4. Viewing the Spotify Year in Review site on a Windows 8 laptop in Internet Explorer

To further verify the issue, I loaded up Chrome Canary, I turned off touch events in *chrome://flags*, and the site suddenly worked. I was on the same machine with a slightly altered version of Chrome (one less event exposed on the `window` object) and suddenly I was "capable" of viewing the content.

Now, I'm a developer and writer with a keen interest in issues of compatibility on the modern Web, so my experience was frustrating but still had a silver lining, as I was able to use the experience here in this book. I also had the tools needed to debug the issue and actually view the content (which was actually rather cool). But what about all the users of Chromebooks and Windows 8 laptops that hit that screen and didn't have a vested interest in trying to figure out what was going on? There is no silver lining. It was just frustrating.

If they were really interested in providing a separate solution for small-screen mobile devices, they should have used one of the redirect schemes we talked about in Chapter 4 and actually targeted attributes of mobile devices rather than inferring a mobile device from a property of the `window` object. There's nothing wrong with providing dedicated mobile experiences; you just need to do it correctly, and inferring "mobile" from `if (Monderizr.touch)` isn't the correct way to do it.

You Can Fail Just a Little

For a less catastrophic example, take a look at the galleries on wired.com on a touch-enabled laptop. I discovered rather quickly that the previous and next arrows that are circled in Figure 5-5 don't work on a click event fired on a touch-enabled laptop.

Figure 5-5. Nonfunctional buttons on a touch-enabled laptop

Looking at the code (*http://bit.ly/uw-wired-code*), it's clear that they're treating the choice of touch or no-touch as purely binary. Using a ternary operator, they're creating an event alias `touchity`, which uses basically the same test as Modernizr.touch to set the event name as `touchstart` on browsers with touch capability and `click` on everything else:

```
var touchity = (('ontouchstart' in window) ||
(window.DocumentTouch
&&
document instanceof DocumentTouch)) ? 'touchstart' : 'click';
```

So, later on, when events are bound and `touchity` is passed into jQuery's `$.on`, under the hood, only `touchstart` or `click` is set:

```
$('.wp35-gallery .nav').add('.curtain').on(touchity, function(e)
{
  autoPlay('forceStop');
  if (isThisADoubleTap()) {
    e.preventDefault();
  }
  if ($(this).hasClass('next')
      || (event.target.id === 'curtain-right')) {
    offsetSlide(1);
  } else {
    offsetSlide(-1);
  }
});
```

We'll look at technical best practices for how to handle this kind of a thing in a later section, but for now just know that if `click` isn't fired, my mouse isn't going to work. That's frustrating. It's also a serious accessibility concern as keyboard-initiated events won't fire. Even pure "touch" devices like the iPhone or many Android phones can be paired with a keyboard or mouse and will, in many cases, only fire a `click` event.

The rest of this chapter will help you avoid these kind of mistakes.

Design for a Spectrum of Potential User Inputs

This section will cover some of the ways you can improve your designs to better serve the wide variety of user inputs available. Thinking about the breadth of known devices and trying to stay open to new inputs will stop you from inadvertently shutting the door on a potential customer.

Lean Toward Finger-Friendly Interfaces for All Interfaces

If you design for touchscreens and provide large hit areas for buttons, you will make life easier for touchscreen users and users with a mouse or other precise inputs won't be adversely affected by having a large hit area.

Everyone wins.

Touch Target Sizes

44px is the standard size for iPhone buttons. This is based on the size of a human thumb. It has become the de facto standard for "touch-friendly" buttons. You can move up and down from this number, but it's a safe baseline from which to work. Serve the same-sized buttons to everyone.

If you make an interface that is usable for touch, it will be usable with a mouse. Design for the purpose of the site. You don't have to design for a specific form factor or display.

If you're using a dedicated mobile experience, this won't change anything for you, as you're likely already providing a nice fat hit area. It's on the large-screen experience where you'll need to make changes in the way you approach design, lowering the information density overall and using larger interface elements.

Don't Rely on Hover

Hover effects can be an enhancement, but they shouldn't be the only way to get at content or functionality. You should already be aware of this as an area of concern because keyboard users require focus events in addition to mouse events to activate hover content, but this is an even greater concern than the keyboard user. You *can* activate this content with a long press on touch-only devices, but that's a workaround for behavior that needs to be rethought in general. If you're going to hide content, make an explicit action to expose it.

Embrace Clarity

When you start to design for touch everywhere, you trade off on the amount of information you can fit on the screen. This can be a good thing. This forces you to make more aggressive decisions about the need for certain features and functionality. Bringing some clarity to your design is a benefit for you and your users.

Working with the Full User Input Spectrum

This section will examine the technical aspects of working with user input. You will learn how the events you're familiar with, like click, work with the touch events we've discussed to allow interaction with the user. You'll also learn about the new pointer events model, which

I, and many others, want to be the model to take us into the future of event handling in the browser (even if the path of that future is unclear at present).

The Current State of Touch and Mouse Event Handling

Learning the intricacies of how this works from an event-handling perspective is important. Although I hope that we'll have a more streamlined event system for user input available in the future, dealing with the full spectrum of touch and mouse events is, for now, a requirement for every developer looking to properly handle interactions on the modern Web.

Masters of the Touch Research Universe

Basically everything I know about this I learned from these three sources: the Modernizr project, Peter Paul Koch (*http:// quirksmode.org/*), and Patrick H. Lauke (*https://www.splin tered.co.uk/*). If you want to know everything there is to know about this stuff, then keep those three sources on your radar.

Let's look at the different components of this issue. From the plain fact that you can do nothing to the more advanced ways to manage the variety of user input, this section should get you up and running with modern event handling.

You don't have to do anything new

As long as you're not relying too heavily on hover events (mouseover and mouseout), and you're not doing anything that tracks the mouse's movements (mousemove), you don't need to do anything to have a broadly compatible site or application. Smartphones and tablets were launched onto a Web that wasn't specifically tuned for touch, so they *all* mimic traditional mouse events. The following code sample represents a basic event spy that reports back the mouse and click events that are performed on an element:

```
<!DOCTYPE html>
<html>
  <head>
    <meta charset="utf-8">
    <link rel="stylesheet" href="spy.css">
  </head>
  <body>
    <div id="spy"><p>Tap here</p></div>
```

```
<div id="reporter"></div>
<script>
  window.addEventListener('DOMContentLoaded', function() {
    var events = [
    'touchstart','touchmove','touchend','touchenter',
    'touchleave', 'touchcancel', 'mouseover',
    'mousemove','mouseout', 'mouseenter','mouseleave',
    'mousedown','mouseup','focus','blur','click'
    ];
    for (var i=0; i<events.length; i++) {
      document.getElementById("spy")
        .addEventListener(events[i], function(e){
        document.getElementById("reporter")
          .innerHTML += "<p>"+e.type+"</p>"
        }, false);
      }
    }, false);
  </script>
  </body>
</html>
```

Figure 5-6 shows the events reported when a finger taps the event spy element on Chrome in Windows 8.

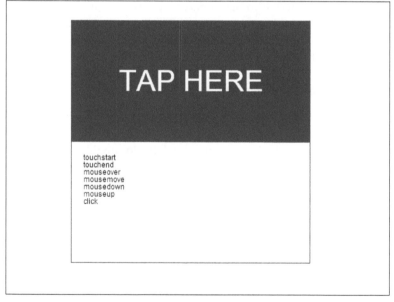

Figure 5-6. Events reported by Chrome on Windows 8

First, we have two touch events (`touchstart` and `touchend`) and then a series of faked mouse events (`mouseover`, `mousemove`, `mousedown`, `mouseup`, and `click`). You can see how much of what you've coded for the mouse still works, as a full set of mouse-based events are faked and fired. There is only one `mousemove` event fired, so as I mentioned, if you're tracking the mouse for some sort of animation or game play that won't work, but otherwise, many basic operations are going to work without you having to lift a finger.

For a further illustration of the pitfalls of trying to tie this down to a binary proposition (because I can't stress that point enough), I did an interesting test with the pen on the Samsung Galaxy Note 2. As you can see in Figure 5-7, there are multiple `mousemove` events fired in addition to the touch events and simulated click event fired in typical touch events. This is because the stylus can interact with the screen even before it touches the surface, and while it does have contact with the surface, it's tracked just like a mouse.

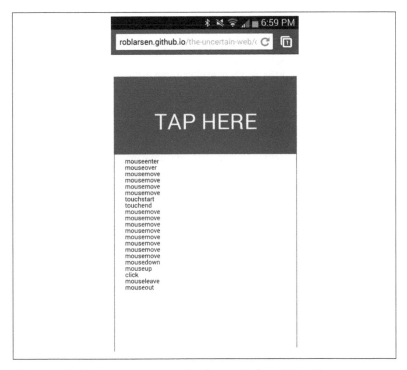

Figure 5-7. Mousemove events fired on a Galaxy Note II

This still would "just work" and would actually work with mouse move events where touchmove would not, but it just goes to show how difficult it is to identify a "touch" device. If I were using this as a phone and then pulled out the stylus midstream, I would suddenly have a "mouse" with hover events and multiple mousemove events. As soon as the stylus went back in, the "mouse" would be gone.

One major catch: There's a 300ms delay on compatibility click events

There is a problem with just binding to click events and wiping your hands of the whole mess. There's a 300ms delay built into the firing of the simulated, compatibility click events that we learned about earlier in the chapter. This is due to the fact that browsers need to wait to see whether or not you're doing a double-tap. The double-tap zooms the screen and is an important enhancement for compatibility and accessibility. The following code sample illustrates this by doing a crude timer between the firing of a touchstart event and the simulated click event:

```html
<!DOCTYPE html>
<html lang="en">
  <head>
    <meta charset="utf-8">
    <link rel="stylesheet" href="spy.css">
  </head>
  <body>
    <div id="spy"><p>Tap here</p></div>
    <div id="reporter"></div>
    <script>
      window.addEventListener('DOMContentLoaded', function() {
        var now, later;
        document.getElementById("spy")
          .addEventListener('touchstart', function(){
            now = Date.now();
        }, false);
        document.getElementById("spy")
          .addEventListener('click', function(){
            later = Date.now();
            document.getElementById("reporter")
              .innerHTML += "<p>Delay:"+(later-now)+"ms</p>"
        }, false);
      }, false);
    </script>
  </body>
</html>
```

The timing works out to at least a 300ms delay on a Samsung Galaxy Note II (Figure 5-8). There's a bit of overhead in the processing of the times, and there are multiple events fired in between the `touchstart` and `click` events, which accounts for the extra few milliseconds.

Figure 5-8. Showing the 300ms delay between the touchstart and click events

This is a noticeable delay, so it can hinder the perceived responsiveness of your site if you don't manage it properly. There are two different ways to manage this delay.

For starters, the browsers themselves have started to suppress the delay if the page is not able to be zoomed by the user. Adding the `view port` meta element with a value of `user-scalable=no` in Firefox for Android and `width=device-width` in Chrome 32 or later indicates to the browser that the page shouldn't be scalable with double-tap and the delay will be suppressed.

User Scaling Is a Feature

user-scalable=no suppresses all zooming, not just double-tap to zoom. This means you lose the ability to zoom the page with pinch-zoom as well. This is a serious accessibility and usability concern. If you go this route, you have to ensure that you're serving content that is going to be readily legible by visually impaired users.

This technique isn't supported in iOS or on Windows Phones, so even if you can safely take advantage of this, you need to look at other options to enhance your site performance.

The second option is to bind actions to *both* click and touchstart, which ensures that touchscreen devices fire the event as soon as possible (touchstart), while still supporting the broadest range of devices with widely compatible click events still bound. You do need to call the preventDefault method of the event object in order to stop the function from being called multiple times. As you've already learned, touch devices call a number of events when a screen is tapped, and if you've bound the same function to two or more of them, the function will be called multiple times.

An example of how this can go wrong can be seen in the following code sample. The function toggles the presence of a class, "toggled," on the spy element. Tapping the screen with a finger visibly fires the function twice (visible because of the 300ms delay, of course), turning the element light brown and then back to the original blue in quick succession:

```
<!DOCTYPE html>
<html lang="en">
  <head>
    <meta charset="utf-8">
    <link rel="stylesheet" href="spy.css">
  </head>
  <body>
    <div id="spy"><p>Tap here</p></div>
    <div id="reporter"></div>
    <script>
      window.addEventListener('DOMContentLoaded', function() {
        function beltAndSuspenders(e){
          if (this.className === "toggled"){
            this.className="";
          } else {
            this.className = "toggled";
```

```
      }
      document.getElementById("reporter")
        .innerHTML += "<p>"+e.type+"</p>"
    }
    document.getElementById("spy")
      .addEventListener('touchstart',
                         beltAndSuspenders, false);
    document.getElementById("spy")
      .addEventListener('click', beltAndSuspenders, false);
  }, false);
</script>
</body>
</html>
```

To fix this, you use the e.preventDefault method (where e represents the event object passed in automatically to the function) in the bel tAndSuspenders function. This stops multiple events from firing and allows you to suppress the click delay on an element safely:

```
function beltAndSuspenders(e){
  e.preventDefault();
  if (this.className === "toggled"){
    this.className="";
  } else {
    this.className = "toggled";
  }
  document.getElementById("reporter")
    .innerHTML += "<p>"+e.type+"</p>"
}
```

Using this ensures that the function will only fire once, and the spy element will remain light brown.

Use preventDefault Sparingly

event.preventDafault should only be used on specific interface elements and not on the body or other parent element. Using event.preventDafault in a function bound to touchstart will kill the default scroll-by-touch and pinch-to-zoom behaviors. This is a major accessibility and usability concern. Suppressing the click delay is great, but not at the expense of users who might need or want a boost in text size.

In addition to these fundamental solutions, there's a small library called FastClick (*https://github.com/ftlabs/fastclick*), from the *Financial Times*, which allows you to simplify the suppression of the click delay across an entire page safely. Using it is a snap. Insert the script into the page, and then FastClick intercepts all touch interactions on

the body and triggers an immediate `click` event when it identifies the
need for one:

```html
<!DOCTYPE html>
<html lang="en">
  <head>
    <meta charset="utf-8">
    <link rel="stylesheet" href="spy.css">
  </head>
  <body>
    <div id="spy"><p>Tap here</p></div>
    <div id="reporter"></div>
    <script src="fastclick.js"></script>
    <script>
      window.addEventListener('DOMContentLoaded', function() {
        FastClick.attach(document.body);
        function beltAndSuspenders(e){
          if (this.className === "toggled"){
            this.className="";
          } else {
            this.className = "toggled";
          }
          document.getElementById("reporter")
            .innerHTML += "<p>"+e.type+"</p>"
        }
        document.getElementById("spy")
        .addEventListener('click', beltAndSuspenders, false);
      }, false);
    </script>
  </body>
</html>
```

At present, FastClick is the recommended path for handling click
events across devices.

Working with the *move events

Working with `mousemove` and `touchmove` events is handled similarly
to the way `click` and `touchstart` are handled, with some slight ad-
justments to deal with the potential to have multiple touchpoints
(multiple fingers equals the potential for 10 touches) on the screen.
The following code sample creates a simple canvas demo that will allow
you to draw on the screen using randomly colored circles. The demo
follows your finger or mouse and plots a trail of circles using the x-
and y-coordinates of your mouse or finger on the screen.

Like the previous `click` and `touchstart` example, this demo listens
for both `mousemove` and `touchmove` events on a `canvas` element. Like

the previous example, bubble uses e.preventDefault to stop other events from firing. Following that is the one major difference between this and the click/touchstart example. The function tests to see if e.touches is available. If it is, it's a touch event, and in this case at least, we just access the first touch and get the e.clientX and e.clientY of the event, which we use to set the x and y of the circle.

e.clientY and e.clientX

e.clientY and e.clientX are event properties that indicate the x and y position of the event from the upper-left corner of the screen. If this canvas element were offset slightly from the top left, we'd have to take into account the offset of the element itself for these coordinates to make sense.

If there is no e.touches, then we simply get the e.clientY and e.clientX of the single mousemove event directly:

```html
<!DOCTYPE html>
<html lang="en">
  <head>
    <meta charset="utf-8">
    <link rel="stylesheet" href="spy.css">
  </head>
  <body>
    <canvas id="track" width="1024" height="768"></canvas>
    <button id="reset">Reset</button>
    <script>
      window.addEventListener('DOMContentLoaded', function() {
        var canvas = document.getElementById("track"),
            ctx = canvas.getContext("2d");
        function randomHex(){
          return '#'+ Math.floor(Math.random()*16777215)
                      .toString(16);
        }
        function circle( params ) {
          params = params || {};
          var x = params.x,
              y = params.y,
              radius = params.radius || 10,
              fillStyle = params.fillStyle || false;
          ctx.moveTo( x, y );
          ctx.beginPath();
          ctx.arc( x, y, radius, 0, 2 * Math.PI);
          if ( fillStyle ) {
            ctx.fillStyle = fillStyle;
            ctx.fill();
          }
```

```
        ctx.closePath();
      }
      function bubble(e){
        e.preventDefault();
        var x,y;
        if (e.touches){
          x = e.touches[0].clientX;
          y = e.touches[0].clientY;
        } else {
          x = e.clientX;
          y = e.clientY;
        }
        circle({
            x:x,
            y:y,
            radius:20 * Math.random(),
            fillStyle:randomHex()
        });
      }
      canvas.addEventListener('mousemove', bubble, false);
      canvas.addEventListener('touchmove', bubble, false);
        document.getElementById("reset")
        .addEventListener('click', function(){
          ctx.clearRect( 0, 0, 1024, 768 );
        }, false);
    }, false);
  </script>
 </body>
</html>
```

Writing my first name with my finger produces the following result. Play around with the demo (Figure 5-9). It's fun.

As you might have inferred from the presence of the `e.touches` array in the previous example, handling multiple touches is also possible.

Multitouch Events Are "Touch-Only" Interactions
As soon as there are two or more touch events at one time, only the touch events are fired. Mouse compatibility events are suppressed. This makes sense if you think about it because there's really no way to model a multitouch interaction with traditional mouse events.

Figure 5-9. The output of drawing with a finger on the screen

This example expands on the previous one to support multiple touches. If e.touches is available, instead of getting the first one and getting the coordinates of a single event, we loop through the entire e.touch es array and draw a circle for each of the touches present:

```html
<!DOCTYPE html>
<html lang="en">
  <head>
    <meta charset="utf-8">
    <link rel="stylesheet" href="spy.css">
  </head>
  <body>
    <canvas id="track" width="1024" height="768"></canvas>
    <button id="reset">Reset</button>
    <script>
      window.addEventListener('DOMContentLoaded', function() {
        var canvas = document.getElementById("track"),
            ctx = canvas.getContext("2d");
        function randomHex(){
          return '#'+ Math.floor(Math.random()*16777215)
                           .toString(16);
        }
        function circle( params ) {
          params = params || {};
          var x = params.x,
              y = params.y,
              radius = params.radius || 10,
```

```
        fillStyle = params.fillStyle || false;
      ctx.moveTo( x, y );
      ctx.beginPath();
      ctx.arc( x, y, radius, 0, 2 * Math.PI);
      if ( fillStyle ) {
        ctx.fillStyle = fillStyle;
        ctx.fill();
      }
      ctx.closePath();
    }
    function bubble(e){
      e.preventDefault();
      var x,y;
      if (e.touches){
        for (var i = 0,
            len = e.touches.length;
            i < len; i++){
          x = e.touches[i].clientX;
          y = e.touches[i].clientY;
          circle({
            x:x,
            y:y,
            radius:20 * Math.random(),
            fillStyle:randomHex()
          });
        }
      } else {
        x = e.clientX;
        y = e.clientY;
        circle({
          x:x,
          y:y,
          radius:20 * Math.random(),
          fillStyle:randomHex()
        });
      }
    }
    canvas.addEventListener('mousemove', bubble, false);
    canvas.addEventListener('touchmove', bubble, false);
    document.getElementById("reset")
      .addEventListener('click', function(){
        ctx.clearRect( 0, 0, 1024, 768 );
      }, false);
    }, false);
  </script>
  </body>
  </html>
```

Drawing a star with two fingers produces the following output (Figure 5-10).

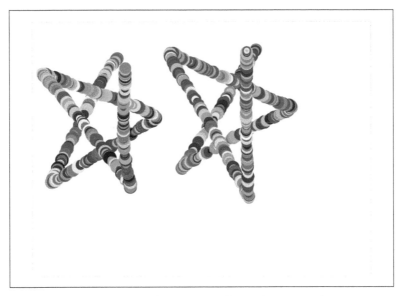

Figure 5-10. The output of drawing with two fingers on the screen

Now that we've seen the current state of mouse and touch, let's look at a new simplification of these interactions available starting with Microsoft Internet Explorer 10 and hopefully coming to other browsers soon.

Pointer events: One event model for mouse, touch, and more

Starting with Internet Explorer 10, Microsoft introduced the Pointer Events model for handling user input. Pointer Events has since moved to be a W3C specification (*http://www.w3.org/TR/pointerevents/*). Pointer Events is modeled after traditional mouse events, except they use the concept of a pointer to apply one model across all user input, including mouse, touch, and pen. This allows you to write a single set of events that work across hardware capabilities. Instead of binding functions to mousemove and touchmove, you simply bind to pointer move and run one function for any input. No matter what input device appears in the future, your pointer event will fire as long as the browser and operating system correctly report the input.

Table 5-1 maps the common mouse events to their corresponding pointer event.

Table 5-1. Mouse events mapped to pointer events

Mouse Event	Pointer Event
mousedown	pointerdown
mouseenter	pointerenter
mouseleave	pointerleave
mousemove	pointermove
mouseout	pointerout
mouseover	pointerover
mouseup	pointerup

The pointer event has all the familiar properties you expect from mouse events. This makes using Pointer Events pretty straightforward. With one small CSS-based addition, the code we've been working with to draw randomly colored bubbles is simplified greatly by using Pointer Events. For example, there's no need to fork based on the event type. There's also no need to loop through a collection of touches because each pointer event is handled independently. Looking at just the bubble function, you can see that it's now down to one line. All you need to do is access the clientY and clientX of the pointer event and pass it into the circle method:

```
function bubble(e){
  circle({
    x:e.clientX,
    y:e.clientY,
    radius:20 * Math.random(),
    fillStyle:randomHex()
  });
}
```

The CSS addition is a single property touch-action, which indicates whether or not default touch actions should be performed on the element:

```
canvas {
  -ms-touch-action: none;
  touch-action: none;
}
```

As I mentioned, Pointer Events (*http://bit.ly/uw-w3-pointer*) are being standardized by the W3C. They're currently a candidate recommendation, which is pretty far down the road to standardization. They're currently only supported by IE10 and IE11, but Firefox Nightly now exposes this functionality with the option `dom.w3c_point er_events.enabled`.

For a long time, Chrome had considered adding support for Pointer Events (*http://bit.ly/uw-chrome-pointer*). In August 2014, they reversed course and announced that they wouldn't be moving forward with an implementation, even behind a flag. Instead, they would look to solve the problem of user input on the Web with "extensions" to the existing touch events.

Whatever that means.

Safari has also stated they won't support them, but the hope was that with Chrome, Firefox, and Internet Explorer adding support, Safari would come along for the ride. Similar "peer pressure" had worked with WebGL after all (where Internet Explorer was the odd man out).

This state of events is unfortunate, as I believe this event model is superior to the current hybrid model we've got.

There is a *chance* that Google will reconsider its decision based on the stars and discussion on the Chromium Issue (*http://bit.ly/uw-chrome-pointer*), but as of right now, we're at an impasse in terms of browser support for Pointer Events.

Confusion Ahead

There was, unfortunately, a similarly named, but entirely separate, CSS specification named Pointer Events (*http://wiki.csswg.org/spec/css4-ui#pointer-events*), which indicates whether or not an element should receive click/hover events. You may find both if you search for this topic. At present, the majority of the useful links are either from Microsoft or Patrick H. Lauke's many presentations and articles, so if you're looking at one of their links, you're probably on the right track.

If you're interested in working with Pointer Events, there's a now deprecated but still useful polyfill for Pointer Events from Google's Polymer Project (*http://bit.ly/uw-polymer-pointer*). Once you've gotten your hands on the script (the Polymer Project recommends the use of Bower (*http://bower.io/*) to install the script, but you can also just download it from this chapter's code samples (*http://bit.ly/uw-pointer-polyfill*)), it's as simple as including *pointerevents.js*:

```
<script src="pointerevents.min.js"></script>
```

...and then setting the `touch-action` attribute on the canvas element. `touch-action="none"` indicates that Polymer should listen to all events and not fire scroll events in any direction:

```
<canvas id="track"
  width="1024" height="768"
  touch-action="none"></canvas>
```

This adds Pointer Event support to Chrome 18+, Safari 6+, IE 10, and Firefox 14+.

Assume Nothing and Accommodate Everyone

Whatever method you choose to handle user input—ignoring touch entirely and just relying on compatibility events, handling multiple events, or looking to the future and supporting Pointer Events—the one constant is that you shouldn't think about users as being "touch users" or "mouse users." Your users can and will have multiple inputs on the same device and even in the same session. You shouldn't gate your site based on what you assume about the input configuration of your users' devices. Instead, although you can and should take advantage of advanced inputs to provide novel interfaces, you should provide a solid baseline that takes advantage of the compatibility and accessibility functionality built into the web platform, web browsers, and devices.

CHAPTER 6

The Surprisingly Complex World of Images on the Web

> The world today doesn't make sense,
> so why should I paint pictures that do?
>
> — Pablo Picasso

More than 20 years after Mark Andreesen first proposed the `img` element (*http://bit.ly/uw-img-tag*), the image remains the most direct route from the designer's imagination to the user's screen. Sure, with CSS we have many powerful tools to execute designs, but nothing in our arsenal can compare to the power of art, illustration, and photography in regards to telling a story on the Web. The Web is just a new front for the display of the power of the image. The power of painting and visual art can be seen in the throngs of people that visit the great museums of the world on any given day (Figure 6-1) and the Web taps into the same power.

With this innate power, the continued growth of the size of desktop displays, the increasing quality of displays across form factors, and a design trend toward large, evocative images have all conspired to push the image formats and markup tools we have now to their breaking point.

Add in the vagaries of mobile bandwidth, and all of a sudden, the landscape for images on the Web is more complicated than it's ever been. It's still the best way to tell a story, but trying to thread the needle between the best possible performance (serving the smallest possible image over the fastest connection) while also pleasing the owners of high-density displays (which require much larger image sizes) has been an ongoing issue for several years. The demands of responsive web design (RWD) have also served to complicate matters, as designers are interested in using different images entirely depending on certain aspects of the user's browser.

We've started to solve some of these issues and are making progress toward solving them all.

Figure 6-1. The power of image is so great that we'll wait in lines to see the world's art

As I mentioned in Chapter 4, there are server-side options for enhancing RWD implementations. In a RESS-type system, at the template level, a content management system (CMS) might test against a known set of device characteristics and serve adjusted image elements or entirely different/dynamically created files as needed. There are also fancy CDN-based solutions, which will optimize images based on browser and device characteristics, as well as potential bandwidth.

The innate scalability of Scalable Vector Graphics (SVG) has also begun to make a comeback. Because the SVG format is based on a series of rendering instructions delivered to the browser in text format and not specific pixel information, browsers can scale SVG without increasing file sizes or bandwidth costs.

In addition to these solutions, there are new options on the horizon. Thanks to some incredible work by the full web technology community (developers, standards folks, and browser vendors), we've now got a new picture element, an associated source element, and new img attributes that will allow us to handle these use cases in the browser.

If it sounds like a lot to take in, you're right. If there's one issue that requires flexibility and a solid understanding of the tools available to smooth out the uncertainty, it's this one. The rest of this chapter will go through the different issues at play and will look at the technical solutions that are here for us to use now, as well as those that will help solve these problems in the future.

While We Weren't Paying Attention, Images Got Complicated

As I mentioned in the intro, images on the Web are pretty old. They're also vitally important. Without the introduction and wholesale adoption of images, the Web would have remained a text-based academic novelty. With images, we got everything from millions of GeoCities fan sites to Amazon (all the better to sell products) and everything else that has followed. Images were a vital component of the Web taking the world by storm.

Technically, images were, up until a few years ago, also very well understood. While I'll admit I've written an entire book chapter on images, that depth came down to how important they are, not to how complex they are in practice. The basics of the img element are easy to understand. You have an img element. You give it an src that points to an image somewhere on the Web and an alt attribute that provides textual context of the image, and that's all you need to get a picture of a cat on the Web. It was that way for a long time. With the exception of one small panic when there was a threat of Unisys clobbering the Web with its GIF-related patent (*http://bit.ly/uw-gnu-gif*), we pretty much settled into a period of 10 or 15 years where images were as constant as the seasons.

Then, a few years ago, things started to change.

For one thing, people simply started using larger images. The example I always point to is Boston.com's Big Picture (*http://www.boston.com/bigpicture/*) blog. It presents 30–40 large images on a single topic with minimal commentary. The thing that was great about it when it launched was that the images were large. They were output to fill a 1024-pixel screen. These days it's common (*http://bit.ly/uw-lg-photo*) to find sites that use full-width imagery that stretches well beyond 1024 pixels, but sites like the Big Picture really drove that trend. When it launched, it was a novelty.

This trend comes with a price. Steve Souders has identified this as a major factor in the web performance space. As Figure 6-2 (generated with data from the HTTPArchive (*http://httparchive.org/*)) shows, the average size of web pages has ballooned recently. The majority of those bytes are in images.

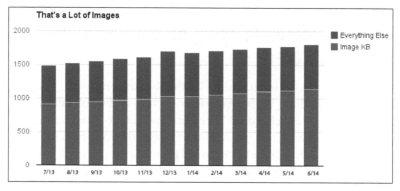

Figure 6-2. The progression of web page sizes

This is an exciting trend from a visual perspective, but it brings with it concerns over bandwidth and performance. All those pixels have to come down the wire. This is especially troubling when you factor in mobile bandwidth. Getting all those bytes down to a user on a crappy mobile connection is tough, and people are paying for those bytes as part of their monthly plan or pay-as-you-go system. Because of this trend, and because of the overall growing interest in web performance, there's been a lot of discussion about how to best optimize images for the Web and how to serve them as efficiently as possible.

This discussion is complicated by both the design demands of RWD and the need to serve higher resolution versions of images in order to "wow" the audience on high-pixel density displays.

A Matter of Semantics

You're probably thinking—didn't we already see an example of using different images at different resolutions and different crops when we initially talked about RWD? We did. There, however, we used CSS background images. This larger issue is about the primary content images you would see in a news site, blog, or shopping site. These images are primary content, will be implemented in the DOM as elements on their own, and need to use standard markup in order to fit into the existing infrastructure of screen readers, search engines, browsers, and content management systems.

The following section lays out some of the major factors that have come into play with images over the past few years. Not so long ago, the first was our only concern. How things have changed. This is the landscape we're attempting to navigate in this chapter.

We Want to Serve the Smallest Possible File Size

This is really the core issue. It just manifests itself in many ways. In a perfect world, we would only ever send the smallest possible number of bytes needed to render the image at an acceptable quality level. Failing a new, adaptive image format, that might not be possible, but it's still something that we can improve upon with new markup, tooling, and awareness of the issue.

We Need to Take Advantage of the Browser Preloader

All modern web browsers use a technique where the browser skips ahead, while simultaneously reading through the document and building out the DOM, and reads through the document looking for additional assets that it can go ahead and start to download. If, for example, you've got a data table that might take hundreds of milliseconds to render, this preloading can help as an image or JavaScript file later in the DOM can start to download even while the browser is still reading and rendering the complicated table markup. Ilya Grigorik of Google says this can improve performance up to 20%. (*http://bit.ly/uw-preloader*) For performance's sake, therefore, it's important that any image solution you use can take advantage of the preloader. This means you should look to semantic, markup-based solutions wherever possible.

We Want to Serve Correctly Sized Images to Multiple Resolutions

If you're serving a "big" image to a 2048-pixel monitor, then you want it to be a "big" image—1600px or more. A big image on a tablet or phone, on the other hand, might only need to be 320 or 480 pixels wide. Sending the correct amount of data in this case can significantly improve performance.

We Need to Serve the Correct Image for Multiple Pixel Ratio Devices

To produce clean images on devices with a high device pixel ratio, you need to send down proportionally larger files than are displayed for a given set of CSS pixels. Images that are crisp on a standard desktop display would show artifacts on a high-pixel density display. Obviously, you can just send higher resolution images to all browsers, but those pixels come at a bandwidth price, so it's much better to just send the correct images to the correct devices.

We Want to Choose Different Sizes/Images at Different Breakpoints

There is a desire to be able to show different images for different orientations and screen resolutions. On a large screen, in an article describing flora in Tucson, Arizona, you might use a wide image that shows a variety of the hardy plant life you can find there. On a small screen in portrait orientation, where the impact of the variety would be lost because it would display an inch high with little detail, an image of a Saguaro cactus with a strongly vertical aspect ratio might be a better choice (Figure 6-3).

We Want to Use Design Breakpoints

Plenty of development these days is based around the concept of media query breakpoints. They're one of the primary technologies at the heart of RWD. Images need to be controlled alongside all the other design changes that occur in a responsive site.

Figure 6-3. An illustration of using art direction on the Web

Serving the Correct Format

If you're looking to take advantage of Google's new WebP image format, you need to be able to easily serve WebP images to browsers that support them and serve PNGs or JPEGs to browsers that don't.

Images Are Easy, and They Should Stay Easy

From an authoring perspective, images are dead easy. If possible, the solutions we look at should remain easy to use. The most powerful tools are worthless if they're not easy to implement. This has proven to be more difficult than you might imagine.

Optimizing Images for the Web

Before we fully unravel the complexity of responsive images, it's worth taking a quick look at the basics of serving images over the Web. This includes a look at the common image types and how they fit into the web image toolbox. Many developers still just take whatever a designer gives them for image assets without taking the time to properly optimize these images for web delivery. The first part of optimization is simply ensuring that the correct formats are chosen. Let's look at the common image formats and how and when they should be used.

JPEG

The Joint Photographic Experts Group (JPEG) format was developed to store and compress images such as photographs that require a wide range of colors. When you export a JPEG, you specify by how much you want to compress the image. The process to compress a JPEG involves discarding color data that people would not normally perceive. Because the format discards this data, the data is lost. The original cannot be re-created from a compressed version. JPEGs are therefore referred to as having *lossy compression*.

JPEGs remain the workhorse format for photographs and full-color artwork on the Web. The combination of universality in authoring and rendering, well-established tools for compression, and decent blend between file size and quality have ensured that JPEGs are the first choice for full-color artwork.

Progressive JPEGs

There are two types of rendering schemes for JPEGs. One, *baseline*, renders the entire image from left to right, top to bottom at the highest possible quality. If you watch a large image render in a browser, you can see a baseline image snap into place as it downloads. *Progressive* rendering, on the other hand, renders the image in several passes of increasing quality.

In the 1990s, we would use progressive JPEGs because any image of reasonable size and quality was going to end up taking a million years to render on most connections. Progressive rendering presented the best *perceived* performance. Now that we're once again dealing with dial-up era speeds in some cases on mobile devices, progressive JPEGs (*http://bit.ly/uw-prog-jpegs*) have made a comeback.

Browsers
Not all browsers (older Internet Explorer and Safari 6 are important exceptions) render progressive JPEGs in the expected way, so not everyone gets the perceived performance benefit. The good news is that browsers that don't render them in the expected way still get the benefit of smaller file size (*http://bit.ly/uw-bookofspeed*) with progressive JPEGs, so it's not a total loss with nonsupporting browsers.

Figure 6-4 shows two versions of the same uncompressed image. One, on the left, is set to baseline rendering. The other, on the right, is set to progressive. You can see the difference as each loads slowly in the browser. The baseline image loads line by line at full resolution. The progressive image, on the other hand, loads a lower resolution version almost immediately and then fills in detail as more data is downloaded.

Figure 6-4. An illustration of progressive rendering versus baseline rendering

Because the full width and height of the image are sketched out by the browser early, the apparent performance is much better. Something that looks relatively complete happens earlier.

GIF

Graphics Interchange Format (GIF) images are created using a palette of up to 256 colors. Each pixel of the image is one of these 256 colors. Every GIF can have a different palette of 256 colors selected from the full true color (24-bit) range of more than 16 million colors. The GIF format stores the palette of colors in a lookup table. Each pixel references the color information in the lookup table rather than directly specifying its own color information. This means that, if many pixels use the same colors, the image doesn't repeat the same color information, which results in a smaller file size. Because of the limited palette, GIFs have been traditionally used for flat graphics like logos or icons rather than photographic images. Because of the popularity of Portable Network Graphics (PNGs), a patent-free alternative to GIF that has gained popularity over the past 10 years, GIFs have fallen out of favor for web production—with the grand exception of *animated* GIFs. Animated GIFs allow you to store multiple frames of an animation in a single file. These low-quality loops have earned a beloved place in the toolbox of goofballs across the Web.

PNG

PNG was developed in the late 1990s in direct response to the Unisys GIF patent controversy mentioned earlier. The PNG format was initially designed for the same use cases as GIF images—basically serving 8-bit flat graphics over the Web. The designers of the format eventually amped it up a little. The 8-bit PNG solves the same problems as an 8-bit GIF, using only 256 colors and on/off transparency, but there is an enhanced 24-bit version of PNG, which has two big advantages:

- Like a JPEG, PNG 24 supports the full true color spectrum.

- A map provides different levels of transparency for every pixel, which allows for softer, anti-aliased edges.

Additionally, PNGs tend to compress to a smaller file size than their GIF equivalent. All of these benefits, mixed with the spark of the GIF patent scare all those years ago, mean that PNG is the format of choice for limited color graphics.

Tooling around PNGs is also excellent, with tools like PNG Crush available to squeeze every last byte out of your images.

SVG

Scalable Vector Graphics are referred to as *vector graphics*. Compared to bitmaps, in which the file contains information about every pixel in the image, vector graphics are defined as mathematical coordinates that define the shapes, paths, text, and other elements that define the image.

As I mentioned in Chapter 2, it's only been over the past few years that they have come to prominence, but SVG images are an excellent option for certain types of graphics. If your site's target audience supports it, or you are willing to build out PNG alternatives for older Android and Internet Explorer, they're a great option. If you work with SVG, you can avoid much of the complexity of the responsive images discussion.

WebP

Offered here as a bit of a novelty for the present, WebP is Google's answer to the question of images on the Web. WebP is a new image format created by the Internet giant that offers significant file size gains over the existing contenders. Google says "WebP is a new image format that provides lossless and lossy compression for images on the Web. WebP lossless images are 26% smaller in size compared to PNGs. WebP lossy images are 25–34% smaller in size compared to JPEG images at equivalent SSIM index."

Sounds great.

Except no one but the Blink browsers are looking to support WebP any time soon. So, although it's an interesting technology to explore and potentially use as an enhancement if you're enterprising, it's not yet ready to replace JPEGs or PNGs. This is especially true because the current tooling for outputting images to WebP isn't as robust as the other common formats. There are a handful of command-line and utility tools available, but WebP support isn't yet in popular authoring programs like Adobe Fireworks or Photoshop without a plug-in, so adoption isn't as easy as telling the production staff to "output WebP" when cutting graphics. It requires automation or the use of a manual utility to get WebP images prepped for the Web.

Choosing the Right File Format

Performance is the driving factor for all of this discussion, so understanding the basics of choosing the right file format is important no matter what choices you end up making with regard to responsive images.

Usually, one or another format will be the obvious choice for you. The rule of thumb is:

- Use JPEGs for photorealistic pictures with a lot of detail or subtle shade differences you want to preserve.

- Use SVG (potentially in concert with PNG fallbacks for older browsers) for images with flat color and hard edges if you're concerned with scaling images across multiple resolutions and don't want to deal with the complexity of the responsive image solutions.

- Use PNGs for images with flat color (rather than textured colors) and hard edges, such as diagrams, text, or logos, and learn the various options for responsive images to deal with scaling images across multiple resolutions.

Obviously, depending on the size and organization of your team, you might have more or less control over this process. If you're a frontend developer responsible for cutting images, then obviously you've got control. If not, and the work is done by a designer or production person on the design team, then it's worth taking some time to train them on the importance of choosing the correct format and choosing output options that best balance the needs of visual clarity with file size.

Additionally, even if you've made the correct choice with the basic file format, there are still some ways in which you can optimize your images using automated tools. This post by Addy Osmani outlines the various options for adding image optimization automation to your process. (*http://bit.ly/uw-img-opt*) If you're not using build automation, learning the various options available to you when you export images for the Web in your software package of choice is invaluable. Using the correct settings at that stage can make a later optimization step redundant.

Look for a CDN Solution

At one point, a CDN solution for images was a real expense and took a lot of technical knowledge to get up and running smoothly. These days, that's not the case. With options like Amazon's Cloudfront out there with example code for every language, a robust ecosystem of tools, and bargain basement prices, the ability to serve your images from geographically optimized locations off fast servers is within the reach of even the most penny-pinching organization.

Definitely try to take advantage of the speed benefits of a CDN. They also allow you to "shard" across different domains, pipelining requests and improving performance. A CDN will be the foundation upon which all your other image delivery enhancements are built.

Responsive Images

Now that we've taken a quick look at the basics of images on the Web, let's look at the extensions to the HTML specifications that have come along over the past few years to solve some of the more advanced use cases outlined previously.

The path to these solutions has been long and occasionally controversial. I'm usually happy to trace the history of web standards development, but the path to `picture`, `srcset`, and `sizes` is so convoluted that it's beyond even my capacity for tracing web dev folklore.

The basic gist is as follows.

As RWD took off, people recognized that the current markup solutions weren't enough to solve the complexities of content images in RWD sites. The `picture` element was proposed in response to this issue. The developer community liked the proposal and began working on honing the solution as a proper specification, working as the Responsive Image Community Group (*http://responsiveimages.org/*) (RICG). The WHATWG and browser vendors didn't end up liking the RICG proposed solution and eventually came up with an alternative proposal, the `srcset` attribute. The developer community was underwhelmed.

Still, because it solved some use cases and browser vendors were amenable to implementation, `srcset` ended up being adopted.

A partial solution is better than no solution at all, of course, but there were still issues--including the file format and art direction use cases outlined earlier.

A couple more years of discussion happened.

Other solutions were proposed.

Eventually... the `picture` element was brought back from the dead, whipped into a form that the WHATWG, browser vendors, and the developer community all liked. `picture` made it into the specification.

The rest of this section will look at these different solutions from a technical perspective.

The Option of Doing Nothing (or Nothing New, at Least)

Before we look at the new-fangled solutions, it is worth pointing out that you solve this to a decent degree without resorting to anything new. With a responsive layout, the use of a little CSS, and images with enough bytes to render decently at higher resolutions, you don't need to do anything using new technology to provide a good *visual* experience for your users across a wide spectrum of devices. This is precisely what I do for my personal, art-heavy blog (*http://javaplusplus plus.com/*). My needs are pretty simple, so I can get away with this approach. I want to scale images between 320 and 800 CSS pixels with additional support for 2x displays.

I output my images at around 1600 pixels, and as a hedge, I pay real attention to using the proper format/settings out of Photoshop. At their worst, these images are 200 KB or so, which isn't bad on a desktop but can be somewhat slow on mobile (Figure 6-5).

Figure 6-5. Bare-bones responsive images on JavaPlusPlusPlus.com

These two lines of CSS will scale the image within its containing block:

```
img {
  max-width: 100%;
  height: auto;
}
```

For my particular use case, this is a "good enough" solution. I'm aware that I'm serving too many bytes to some users, but I'm not at the point where I'm willing to bite the bullet and implement one of the new solutions. At some point, support, tooling, and my own free time will converge to get me to take the plunge, but for right now I'm willing to forgo the optimal solution for one that looks pretty good and takes very little maintenance.

For better or worse, that's still an option for you, too.

srcset

The srcset attribute is a new attribute added to the img element. It can also be used in concert with the picture element, but for now we're going to focus on its original use, which is as an addition to img. Like the standard src attribute, the srcset attribute provides the browser information about the source for the img. Instead of a single image URL, however, the srcset attribute points to a comma-separated list of URLs and associated hints regarding the image size or pixel density. Let's look at an example to understand how those hints work.

For Now, This Is a WebKit and Blink Story

At present, Chrome, Safari, and Opera are the only browsers that support `srcset` out of the box. Firefox has it hidden behind a flag.

In the following code, the `srcset` attribute provides an indication of the device pixel ratio the referenced image should apply to. In this case, there are two options, although you can have as many as you need. First is *more-colors-small.jpg*, which is 600 × 350 pixels wide. It is meant to display at standard resolution. The second image, *more-colors-large.jpg*, is 1200 × 700 pixels and is meant for higher resolution displays. Although it will display at 600 × 350 *CSS* pixels, it's got enough additional image information to look clean in higher resolution devices as well.

The common `src` attribute is still there for browsers that don't understand `srcset`:

```
<!DOCTYPE html>
<html lang="en">
  <head>
    <meta charset="utf-8">
  </head>
  <body>
  <img
    srcset="more-colors-small.jpg 1x,
            more-colors-large.jpg 2x"
    src="more-colors-small.jpg"
    alt="Many colors!"
    width="600" height="350">
  </body>
</html>
```

This is the solution for the device pixel ratio use case. With `src` as a fallback for every browser that supports images, and an `alt` attribute for those that don't, this is a good, backward-compatible solution. Just the way I like it.

To solve more complicated use cases, the `srcset` attribute can work in tandem with the new `sizes` attribute to use media queries to serve separate image sources, displayed with different relative dimensions based on the browser's screen real estate. The following code sample illustrates how this works. It's a little complicated. In fact, all of the remaining examples in this section are a little complicated. Still, these new attributes can be combined in very powerful ways, so it's worth wrapping your head around the complexity.

In this example, the element starts with a src attribute for nonsupporting browsers. In this case, I've chosen a smallish image to ensure that it loads speedily, no matter what device or browser. Following that, there's the new sizes attribute (Blink browsers only at present). sizes accepts a media query/image size pair (or list of pairs). The following illustration (Figure 6-6) breaks down the components. The first part is the media query. This media query should be familiar if you've used them in your CSS. If the query is true, then the image size is set to 60vw. If the media query fails, the size falls back to the default size of 100vw.

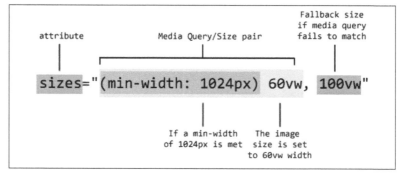

Figure 6-6. The anatomy of a sizes attribute

There can be any number of media query/size pairs. The first one to match wins, and if none match, then the fallback value is used.

The srcset attribute here is more expansive. The list has a series of images between 200 pixels wide and 1600 pixels wide. The second part of the value pair in the source set, instead of indicating the preferred pixel density, hints to the browser the pixel width of the image (200w, 400w, etc.). It's up to the browser to mix and match the best pixel width with the appropriate size at different dimensions and pixel densities:

```
<!DOCTYPE html>
<html lang="en">
  <head>
    <meta charset="utf-8">
  </head>
  <body class="images">
    <img src="more-colors-400.jpg"
      alt="Many colors!"
```

```
      sizes="(min-width: 1024px) 60vw, 100vw"
      srcset="more-colors-200.jpg 200w,
              more-colors-400.jpg 400w,
              more-colors-600.jpg 600w,
              more-colors-1200.jpg 1200w,
              more-colors-1600.jpg 1600w">
  </body>
</html>
```

Personally, I don't find this syntax all that appealing. I don't think the purpose of the long text string inside the srcset attribute is all that apparent without some explanation, and the same goes for the purpose of the sizes attribute. Still, it does the job it was designed to do, so it's worth wrapping your head around the complexity of the syntax. One of these days, you'll want to unlock the power of these new attributes.

sizes sizes

The length part of a size can be specified in any valid CSS length (*http://bit.ly/uw-css-length*), which adds to the possibilities *and* complexity of this attribute. This chapter will stick with vw (viewport width) measurements.

Of course, srcset and sizes are just a complexity appetizer. With the new picture element, both the complexity and the power get amped up. Let's take a look at it in action.

picture

picture was the first solution proposed for responsive images in 2010. This is where the whole epic responsive image standards saga began.

In its original concept (*http://bit.ly/uw-lawson-picture/*), picture was designed as a parallel img element, modeled on the syntax of the HTML5 video and audio elements. The idea was to have a picture element wrapping a series of source elements, which would represent the options for the image source. It would wrap a default img element for nonsupporting browsers. A media attribute on each source would hint to the browser the correct source to use:

```
<picture alt="original proposal">
  <source src="high-resolution.png" media="min-width:1024px">
  <source src="low-resolution.png">
  <img src="low-resolution.png" alt="fallback image">
</picture>
```

For a variety of reasons, this initial proposal was shot down, even after much RICG refinement, because of implementation issues. srcset filled in some of the void, but because it didn't solve all the responsive image use cases, there was always a hole in the specification landscape.

Years passed and eventually, after many false starts, picture was resurrected and reworked to fill that hole.

However, instead of being a replacement for img, picture is now an enhancement *to* the img element to help browsers sort out the best possible solution for the source of an image.

Firefox and Chrome, Sitting in a Tree...
At present, Chrome and Firefox are the only browsers that support picture, and both only do so behind a flag or configuration option. In the near term, Opera, Chrome, and Firefox will all have support out of the box.

Let's take a look at an example (Figure 6-7). Although the srcset examples worked with different resolution versions of the same image, this picture example aims to provide different images for different resolutions. Here, in larger browser windows, an image that is wider than it is tall will be shown.

Figure 6-7. The image that will be displayed on large screens

In browser windows smaller than 1024 pixels, a square image will be used (Figure 6-8).

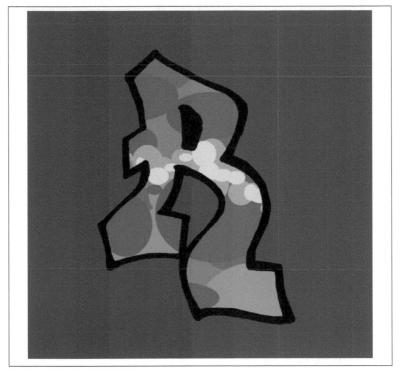

Figure 6-8. The image that will be displayed on small screens

The markup for this is relatively complicated and needs some explaining.

The picture element wraps the entire solution and tells the browser that it's going to be working with this picture element to sort out the source for the child img element. Before we get to that img, there are other elements to work through. The first child element we encounter is the source element. From a developer perspective, source works the way that the original proposal intended. If the media query matches, that source is used. If it doesn't, you move onto the next media query in the stack. Here you have a media query looking for pages with a minimum width of 1024 pixels. If the media query matches, the srcset attribute is used to let the browser choose between three separate source images, ranging from 600 pixels to 1600 pixels wide.

Because this image is intended to be displayed at 50vw, that will give good coverage for the majority of displays. Following that, there's the fallback img element, which also contains a srcset. If the browser doesn't support picture and source or if the previous media queries didn't match, you use the srcset here to get the source for this image. The sizes attribute allows you to further adjust the display for the range of sizes smaller than 1024 pixels:

```
<!DOCTYPE html>
<html lang="en">
  <head>
    <meta charset="utf-8">
  </head>
  <body class="images">
  <picture>
    <source
      media="(min-width: 1024px)"
      sizes="50vw"
      srcset="more-colors-600.jpg 600w,
              more-colors-1200.jpg 1200w,
              more-colors-1600.jpg 1600w">
    <img src="more-colors-square-400.jpg"
      alt="Many colors!"
      sizes="(min-width: 768px) 60vw, 100vw"
      srcset="more-colors-square-200.jpg 200w,
              more-colors-square-400.jpg 400w,
              more-colors-square-600.jpg 600w,
              more-colors-square-800.jpg 800w">
  </picture>
  </body>
</html>
```

It's complicated, but this picture pattern solves the question of both different image sizes and different formats for separate art direction choices.

The following example takes the picture to the limit, combining different sizes, different image formats, *and* art direction in one element. Hopefully, you won't have to get this complex yourself, but if you need to, then this is a pretty good example of how far you can stretch these new elements and attributes.

Prepping WebP Files

The WebP images in the following code were generated using a utility called XNConvert (*http://bit.ly/uw-xnc*). It's cross platform and allows you to quickly create WebP images. If you're committed to using WebP, you'll want to look at automating this process with whatever build system you're using. I am not committed to WebP, so this utility is the way I go when messing around with these things.

The following monster markup block shows how this might be accomplished. It follows the same pattern you just saw with the art direction use case, with the addition of multiple source elements to choose from instead of just one. The first source has a media query looking for displays with a minimum width of 1024 pixels. You've seen that before. The new wrinkle is the addition of the type attribute. If the browser understands how to render image/webp, then it will use that source. With source elements, the order matters, so browsers with larger screens (the matching media query) that support WebP (as indicated by the type attribute) will never get past this source element and will serve an appropriately chosen and sized WebP image to the user.

Just So You Know, the SVG Mime Type Is Image/svg+xml

WebP is used here for the novelty of it, but this feature of picture is also a great option for using SVG while still providing a clean, markup-based fallback for older browsers.

Following that, there is a second source element, which mirrors the srcset and sizes you saw on the img in the previous example. If the minimum width media query fails (the browser is smaller than 1024 pixels), but the browser *does* support the WebP type, this source and srcset will be chosen by the browser. The next source element does the same as the first in the stack, at least in terms of media queries and image sizes, but there is no type attribute. All browsers will use this if they understand picture, source, and srcset, but don't understand the type image/webp. Finally, you have the fallback img element with the default src and small screen srcset:

```html
<!DOCTYPE html>
<html lang="en">
  <head>
    <meta charset="utf-8">
  </head>
  <body class="images">
  <picture>
    <source
      media="(min-width: 1024px)"
      sizes="50vw"
      srcset="more-colors-600.webp 600w,
              more-colors-1200.webp 1200w,
              more-colors-1600.webp 1600w"
      type="image/webp">
    <source
      sizes="(min-width: 768px) 60vw, 100vw"
      srcset="more-colors-square-200.webp 200w,
              more-colors-square-400.webp 400w,
              more-colors-square-600.webp 600w,
              more-colors-square-800.webp 800w"
      type="image/webp">
    <source
      media="(min-width: 1024px)"
      sizes="50vw"
      srcset="more-colors-600.jpg 600w,
              more-colors-1200.jpg 1200w,
              more-colors-1600.jpg 1600w">
    <img src="more-colors-square-400.jpg"
      alt="Many colors!"
      sizes="(min-width: 768px) 60vw, 100vw"
      srcset="more-colors-square-200.jpg 200w,
              more-colors-square-400.jpg 400w,
              more-colors-square-600.jpg 600w,
              more-colors-square-800.jpg 800w">
    </picture>
  </body>
</html>
```

This is likely as complicated as this new markup can be. You can obviously get as granular as you like with the media queries and srcset, but the basic pattern will remain the same, no matter how detailed you get with your designs.

Picturefill, the picture Polyfill

As you've seen, there isn't universal support for these new elements and attributes. Thankfully, the folks at the Filament Group have provided the Picturefill (*http://bit.ly/uw-picturefill*) polyfill, which allows you to use the new responsive markup patterns now, even in browsers that don't support the new elements and attributes. The following code sample shows how easy it is to use Picturefill. You simply need to add the Picturefill script to the head of the document, and because of a bug in Internet Explorer 9 (and only IE9), you need to add a video element wrapping the source elements. This is accomplished using conditional comments, which will only show the video element in IE9:

```html
<!DOCTYPE html>
<html lang="en">
  <head>
      <meta charset="utf-8">
      <script src="picturefill.js"></script>
  </head>
  <body class="images">
  <picture>
    <!--[if IE 9]><video style="display: none;"><![endif]-->
    <source
      media="(min-width: 1024px)"
      sizes="50vw"
      srcset="more-colors-600.jpg 600w,
              more-colors-1200.jpg 1200w,
              more-colors-1600.jpg 1600w">
    <!--[if IE 9]></video><![endif]-->
    <img src="more-colors-square-400.jpg"
      alt="Many colors!"
      sizes="(min-width: 768px) 60vw, 100vw"
      srcset="more-colors-square-200.jpg 200w,
              more-colors-square-400.jpg 400w,
              more-colors-square-600.jpg 600w,
              more-colors-square-800.jpg 800w">
  </picture>
  </body>
</html>
```

The folks at the Filament Group have been involved in the development of these new elements and attributes from their very genesis, so if anyone is going to implement a solid polyfill, it's going to be them.

Because the support for the whole suite of responsive image markup is so spotty at present, you're basically required to use a polyfill solution across the board. As more and more browsers get native support, you would look to test with Modernizr or with your own feature detect for the specific feature you were looking to use and only conditionally load the polyfill as needed at that point.

Embrace SVG

Taking a step back from the markup overload we've seen in the previous section, it's time to look at how SVG can help you with the question of images and the modern Web. As I've mentioned, SVG is vector based and because of that, the information in the file isn't based on pixels but on providing coordinates and instructions embedded in the file in order to create the image. The following is the source of a simple SVG image that creates a pink circle. The `circle` contains a set of instructions as to where to place the center of the circle (cx and cy) and how long the radius (r) should be relative to the SVG elements viewPort:

```
<svg width="200" height="200"
  viewPort="0 0 200 200" version="1.1"
  xmlns="http://www.w3.org/2000/svg">
  <circle cx="100" cy="100" r="75" fill="#fe57a1"/>
</svg>
```

This file can be saved as *circle.svg* and inserted into the document as the `src` of an image:

```
<!DOCTYPE html>
<html lang="en">
  <head>
    <meta charset="utf-8">
  </head>
  <body class="images">
    <img src="circle.svg" width="200" height="200">
  </body>
</html>
```

It will look like Figure 6-9 when rendered in the browser.

That's all pretty straightforward. SVG images can be output from a good, vector-based drawing program like Adobe Illustrator. Considering your designers are already probably using something like Illustrator to create graphics like this means that using SVG might be as easy as having them choose a different export format.

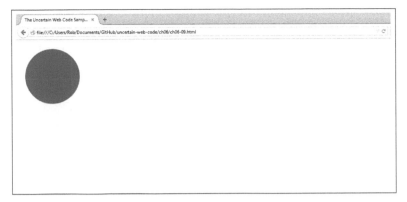

Figure 6-9. A simple SVG example

For the purposes of this chapter and the issue of images on the modern Web, SVG being vector based basically means there's no need to provide different sizes for different resolutions. The browser will take the instructions in the SVG file and render an image that will look good at whatever scale you desire. The instructions like those in the circle element in the previous example are based on the coordinates of the viewPort. If the SVG image scales, its defined viewPort scales and any instructions will scale accordingly.

Take a look at this example, which uses eight separate copies of an SVG image representing the HTML5 logo. The only change in each is the width, as defined in the markup. There is no difference in the rendering quality between any of these images:

```
<!DOCTYPE html>
<html lang="en">
  <head>
    <meta charset="utf-8">
  </head>
  <body class="images">
    <img src="HTML5-logo.svg" width="5%">
    <img src="HTML5-logo.svg" width="10%">
    <img src="HTML5-logo.svg" width="15%">
    <img src="HTML5-logo.svg" width="20%">
    <img src="HTML5-logo.svg" width="25%">
    <img src="HTML5-logo.svg" width="50%">
    <img src="HTML5-logo.svg" width="100%">
    <img src="HTML5-logo.svg" width="200%">
  </body>
</html>
```

As you can see in Figure 6-10, they're crisp all the way up to the 3200-pixel wide rendering of the 200% image. This same power also allows the browser to fill in the gap between CSS pixels and actual pixels in higher pixel density displays.

Figure 6-10. Scaling an SVG image is as easy as changing the dimensions

So, just by switching over to SVG images for more graphical images, you can solve the problem of scaling images up and down based on display size and the issues of pixel density. Not too shabby.

One other nice thing about using SVG is that, instead of just being able to use media queries in your markup to control the display of your images, you can continue to control the display in CSS files where it really belongs.

This example shows how to control the width of the HTML5 logo based on a simple media query (on larger screens, the image will be displayed at 50%, while on smaller screens, it will be displayed at 100%):

```
<!DOCTYPE html>
<html lang="en">
  <head>
    <meta charset="utf-8">
    <style>
     .svg {
       width:100%;
     }
     @media all and (min-width: 1024px) {
       .svg{
         width:50%;
       }
     }
    </style>
  </head>
  <body class="images">
    <img src="HTML5-logo.svg" class="svg">
  </body>
</html>
```

This is, in my mind, far more maintainable than the markup-based solutions. Instead of having to go through the markup to adjust a bunch of sizes attributes if your design changes, you can control the display of these images where they should be controlled--alongside the rest of your design code in your CSS files.

Of course, SVG doesn't solve everything. For starters, there's no support in older IE and Android older than 3.0, so if you're looking to support those browsers you need some scheme to serve PNG versions of these images. For example, you could use picture plus Picturefill, some RESS solution, or simply a script that looks for img elements with an *.svg* extension and replaces them with *.png* in offending browsers. Additionally, there's no markup-based way to properly solve the art direction use case where you want to serve an entirely different image, so if that's important to you, you would be drifting back into the more complicated markup waters. And finally, SVG isn't designed for photographic images, so you're still looking at a markup-based solution for your cat photos.

Still, looking to leverage SVG wherever it makes sense will simplify your life in terms of markup and maintenance, and will produce better quality, no matter what display a supporting browser is running on.

On the Server Side

As we've touched on, there's also the option to handle some of these things on the server side. I'm not going to go into detail because, unlike HTML, CSS, and JavaScript, which we're all in agreement on, there are far too many viable options on the server side for me to be able to present a decent solution that will be easily translatable to everyone's server-side setup.

That said, conceptually the general approaches are pretty easy to understand, no matter what the implementation looks like in your language of choice. There are several ways you can augment your handling of images on the server side.

For example, using one of the mobile detection schemes I talked about, change the HTML template to point to different images based on browser characteristics. Even free CMS solutions like WordPress or Drupal can handle the creation of multiple sizes for images when they're uploaded and expose those sizes through an API, so matching mobile devices to resolutions can happen without *too* much strain. This approach solves whatever use case you have (you can easily swap out whatever image you need for whatever browser) and has the added benefit of being JavaScript agnostic. There's no polyfill needed if you're just rendering the correct image source on the server side and sending it down the pipe correctly.

The downside is, of course, you've split some display logic from the CSS or your markup to your template code, but depending on your team and audience, that might be a trade-off you want to make. If you've got a full-spectrum team with people who are willing to dive in and do some of this heavy lifting on the server side, take advantage of it if it makes sense.

A Practical Developers Guide to All of This Complexity

So, now that you've digested all of this information, and there is a lot of it, what's the best way to approach all of this? Let's review what we've learned so far, and try to put it all together in a way that gives us a foundation for moving forward with images without too much hair-pulling in the future.

Personally, I've looked at this issue with the following factors in mind.

Complexity
How hard is it to implement?

Support
How well will this solution work across browsers and platforms?

Flexibility
Can the solution do what I need to do with responsive images?

Maintainability
How difficult would it be to change the display rules for your site and how much markup is there to sort through?

With those factors in mind, keeping the following points in mind when you launch a new project will help you sort out the right way to go.

Identify How Important Images Are to Your Site

All images on the Web are not created equal. If you're an artist or a photographer, or are working for a global lifestyle brand trying to sell their latest sneakers in Shenzhen, then you've got a lot more interest in providing the best possible quality images all the time than someone merely trying to share a stock image on their "contact us" page.

Get the Basics Right

Outputting images in the correct format, at optimal quality, and at the smallest possible file size gets you a long way toward solving image performance issues. Use a CDN to ensure that the simple geographic spread of your audience isn't causing your hard work to be wasted. There's no point in learning about picture if you're adding a full second to the image download time because you're serving images from your office in New York to your best customer in Australia.

Use the Simplest Possible Solution

If you can, stick to solutions with broad compatibility and lower complexity. With polyfills like Picturefill, it's possible to use picture and srcset now, but with fragmented current browser support, a somewhat uncertain future in browsers (e.g., we haven't even talked about Internet Explorer and there's some question as to whether or not Safari will ship picture, even though the code is already available for Web-Kit), and a specification still in flux (i.e., picture is an "Editor's Draft" at the W3C), you should only wade into the deep end if you really need

---

to. We've reached a really good place in regard to these specifications, but there's still room for some surprises to pop up.

Which isn't to say you shouldn't use `picture` or `srcset` if you really need to. You should, but only as much as you really need to. Don't go straight to `picture` because it's the new and shiny thing when the basic usage of `srcset` will get you to an 85% solution, and, in turn, don't use `srcset` if a well-crafted `img` and vanilla `src` will get you to 85%.

Learn to Love SVG

The simplicity of being able to scale images across multiple break-points with just an `img` element and some CSS is a much easier transition than jumping into `picture` with multiple `source` elements and relying on a polyfill.

Test!

Testing your solutions in real devices with all sorts of connections is going to tell you everything you need to know about where you need to go. Implementing a simple `max-width` solution like I do on my blog might be a "good enough" solution if you test it and find that your images are small enough to load in only a second on a decent mobile connection. Or you might find that the 2 MB image you need to provide high-density pixels for a full-screen background image basically freezes your users' screens and likely causes them to hate you.

There's also the simple fact that all of these technologies, both in the browser and in the polyfill, are pretty new, so you might uncover bugs that were previously unknown. Reporting them makes you a web platform hero.

Conclusion

Images on the Web have gotten more complicated over the years. Large image sizes, performance concerns, and the needs of RWD have combined to make serving images a tricky proposition. By combining a solid understanding of the basics of image optimization, the use of a CDN, an embrace of SVG, and a knowledge of the new markup patterns available, you can solve this complexity right now.

And that's it for this chapter. I've once again written a full book chapter on images; this time, however, it was down to the complexity of the issue. Hopefully, we've reached a complexity plateau for images that will last for at least a few years (if not the next 20).

CHAPTER 7

The Horribly Complex World of Web Video

> Use only that which works, and
> take it from any place you can find it.
>
> — Bruce Lee (as quoted in *Bruce Lee:*
> *Fighting Spirit* by Bruce Thomas)

One of the most important early drivers for adoption of HTML5 was Apple's decision against supporting Adobe Flash on iOS devices. Picking the most important side effect of that decision would be difficult, but one of the biggest was certainly the mad scramble to produce web video that could play on the iPhone. This, of course, meant the HTML5 video element was suddenly important. It was *so* important, for a time at least, that it was common for people to say simply "HTML5" when they were really discussing serving video with the video element.

The thing is, from the first, the video element has been a tricky thing to work with in any practical way. This is strange because at first glance it looks pretty easy to understand, and at its most basic, using the video element *is* straightforward. If you're familiar with the way the replaced elements like img or object (handy for embedding Flash!) work, you will understand how to use video (and audio for that matter.) The associated video API is also simple with easy-to-understand play and pause methods.

If only the *full* story were that simple.

Video is the best current example of a web technology that, because of one factor or another, fails to live up to its promise. Because of that failure, it's much easier to move away from a pure standards-based approach to one that solves the issue in a practical matter. No matter how well designed the element might be, or how easy the API is to use, commercial and technical hurdles make the practical business of web video difficult to manage without a lot of expertise. It's so difficult, in fact, that I'm happy to pass off the video heavy lifting to third parties without a second thought to how technically clean their solution might be.

This chapter will introduce you to web video as it stands and will point out some of the current problems in the landscape. Video is important, so understanding how it works fundamentally is a vital thing for modern web developers and getting a sense of how the third-party services work is also important if you decide to go that way with video in the future. This chapter will show you both how to implement video in a cross-browser way on your own and then will look at how to leverage a couple of different services to use a third party to serve video on the Web.

There will be bumps along the way.

The Core Technology

This section will go through basics of video and will, in turn, look at the many issues that crop up when working with video on the Web. Each of these issues, by themselves, might seem like a reasonable hurdle to overcome.

The *combination* of these is where things start to get a little hairy. As you go through this chapter, start to cross reference the different factors in your head. You'll start to see that, although the basics are not so bad, video as a whole is a tangled mess to do in a world-class way.

The HTML video Element

The video element is the center of this particular circus. With video available, Apple was able to skip Flash support in the iPhone and push people toward a web standards-based video solution instead.

Let's look at the video element in action. The following code sample shows a simple video element with some basic JavaScript-driven interaction. In a supporting browser, this page shows a video of a mechanical cyclist taken at an open air market in Paris along with a simple play/pause toggle button to illustrate controlling the video externally. Figure 7-1 shows what the page looks like in a supporting web browser.

Figure 7-1. The video element in action

In the code, the first important element to note is the video element itself. Like an img element, the video element has an src attribute, which points to a video file. Within the video element, there are also two Boolean attributes. Boolean attributes, which are new to HTML5, are attributes whose mere presence indicates that the value is true. So, instead of saying required=true, you can just write required. The attributes here, controls and autoplay, indicate that there should be controls (play and pause buttons, etc.) in the video interface and that the video should automatically play when the page loads. In addition, there's an id attribute to serve as a hook for the JavaScript function used to control the video.

Accessibility Note

The HTML5 track element is an important accessibility enhancement to online video. Although I am trying to get you to take accessibility seriously, there's no dialogue in this small clip. Therefore, there's no need for subtitles with this video. If you're interested in learning more about how subtitles work with video, check out this succinct article on HTML Rocks (*http://bit.ly/uw-subtitles*).

The JavaScript is pretty simple. First, you get references to the video element and the toggle button using document.getElementById. Then a function is bound to the click event on the toggle element using addEventListener. In the function body, the video.play and video.pause methods are used to play and pause the video depending on the video's current state. The video's current state is tested by accessing the Boolean attribute video.paused.

The final piece of this markup is the fallback content, which lives inside the opening and closing tags of the video element. In this case, the fallback is a paragraph with some text instructing the user to download the video. The assumption with this fallback content is that any phone or computer that doesn't support video in the browser might be able to play the video file in a built-in media player. This is especially important with the proxy browsers, like Opera Mini, which are the likeliest candidates for no video element support on modern mobile devices. If you're familiar with the way noscript works, video fallback content works in much the same way.

We'll figure out sturdier fallback support for older Internet Explorer (the most problematic desktop browser) as we expand on the way that fallback content works throughout the rest of this section:

```html
<!DOCTYPE html>
<html lang="en">
  <head>
    <meta charset="utf-8">
  </head>
  <body class="video">
    <video src="MVI_1749.mp4" controls autoplay
      id="video-sample">
      <p>Your browser can't play HTML5 video.
        <a href="MVI_1749.mp4">Download it</a> instead.</p>
    </video>
    <button id="video-toggle">Pause/Play</button>
    <script>
      var video = document.getElementById("video-sample"),
          toggle = document.getElementById("video-toggle");
      toggle.addEventListener("click", function() {
        if (video.paused) {
          video.play();
        } else {
          video.pause();
        }
      });
    </script>
```

```
    </body>
  </html>
```

That's a clear API. In this case, I think the WHATWG provided a pretty good solution for the markup and DOM API portion of serving video in the browser without the use of a plug-in. It's everything beyond the confines of the specification that has kept us on our toes over the past few years. According to the data from Can I Use? (*http://bit.ly/uw-mpeg4*), the preceding code has full support in only 65% of the world-wide browser market. There are a few different reasons for this gap. You've learned about two (proxy browsers and Internet Explorer 8 and earlier), and you'll learn about the other major one as we make our way through this chapter and build up a decent solution for getting video in a wide range of browsers.

Let's start with the most obvious example, the presence of browsers that don't support the video element at all, but do support Flash. This is Internet Explorer 6–8 and represents the largest single block of nonsupporting browsers out there.

The Flash Fallback

One way to serve video to old browsers is to leverage the fallback content that you saw earlier in precisely the way it was designed. If a browser doesn't understand the video element, it will ignore that element and fall back to whatever is contained within the opening and closing video tags. For Internet Explorer 8 and older, this can be a Flash-based video solution. This works because if the browser understands the video element, the video element itself and any child nodes will be replaced with the browser's video player. If the browser *doesn't* understand video, then the fallback content, in this case a Flash player, will be displayed.

All we need to do with this simple Flash player is pass in the existing source for our video as one of the flashvars and everything just works:

```
<!DOCTYPE html>
<html lang="en">
  <head>
    <meta charset="utf-8">
  </head>
  <body class="video">
    <video src="MVI_1749.mp4" controls autoplay
      id="video-sample">
```

```
<object type="application/x-shockwave-flash"
    width="854" height="504" data="smallplayer.swf"
    classid="clsid:D27CDB6E-AE6D-11cf-96B8-444553540000">
<param name="flashvars" value="videoURL=MVI_1749.mp4">
</param>
<param name="movie" value="smallplayer.swf"></param>
<param name="bgcolor" value="#ffffff"></param>
<param value="true"></param>
<embed type="application/x-shockwave-flash"
    src="smallplayer.swf"
    bgcolor="#ffffff"
    flashvars="videoURL=MVI_1749.mp4"
    width="854" height="504" ></embed>
<p>Your browser can't play HTML5 video.
<a href="MVI_1749.mp4">Download it</a> instead.</p>
</object>
</video>
</body>
</html>
```

This works, but it's not ideal. For starters, we've had to embed that nasty Flash pattern and then, more importantly, we lose easy access to the video DOM API. There are ways to talk to Flash from within Java-Script (I've sure done a lot of it), but talking to both video and Flash requires forking our code in uncomfortable ways.

I'm actually going to table that particular issue for now, although I do promise that I'll have a couple of solutions for you before the chapter is over.

What I'm going to focus on for a bit is making sure that the video itself will play in as many browsers as it can. Because, although we've added support for IE8 and earlier by including Flash, we're still falling short of getting video everywhere we can get it. We're still missing Opera and some versions of Firefox. Why? Well, it's time to learn a little bit about containers and codecs and how they pertain to the latest version of the good old-fashioned browser war.

Containers and Codecs

Simply supporting the video element and related APIs is only half the story for a practical measure of support in browsers. There are two technical components to video that are separate to the standards process, but are fundamental to getting video to the browser: codecs and containers. A *codec*, a portmanteau of *cod*er and *dec*oder, is software that, in this case, translates the video signal to and from the compressed storage format. A *container* is what we think of as a file format.

I'm Intentionally Ignoring Audio

I'm ignoring both the `audio` element and the `audio` codec component of web video. This is partially because I want to keep your heads from exploding. *That* and there are standard audio codecs that pair with each of the video codecs you'll learn about later. Basically, if you don't do anything funky when you export your video, you will end up with a combination of audio codec and video codec that makes sense from a support perspective. So when I talk about MP4, I'm really talking about the h.264 video codec with the AAC audio codec; when I talk about OGM, I'm really talking about the Theora video code with the Vorbis Audio codec; and when I talk about WebM, I'm talking about the VP8 video codec with the Vorbis audio codec.

Have I mentioned this is a rat's nest? *It's a rat's nest.*

So far in our examples, we've seen the MP4 container. Under the hood, that container is paired with the h.264 video codec. This pairing is supported by IE9+, Chrome, Safari, and Firefox on the PC (but *not* Mac or Linux). Because h.264 is a patent encumbered codec, Opera (and for a long time, Firefox on the PC) refused to implement it, instead looking toward open source container/codec combinations like WebM/VP8 and OGG/Theora.

By the way, when I talked about the latest browser war, it was precisely this standoff that I was referring to. For a couple of years, it looked like we would have to work around Firefox's significant market share in perpetuity.

Although Firefox eventually found a way to support MP4/h.264 on the PC (*http://bit.ly/uw-mozilla-h264*), Opera is still a holdout, so we need to tweak our markup to include Opera and non-PC Firefox (as well as Firefox on all platforms prior to version 21).

Adobe Plays Nice with h.264

As you might have surmised from the way we seamlessly passed an MP4 file to the Flash player in our fallback content, Flash has built-in support for MP4/h.264.

In the previous example, there was an `src` attribute directly on the `video` element. In this new example, you'll leverage the same `source` attribute you saw with the `picture` element in the previous chapter.

video works the same way. The first source element that a supporting browser can play will be used as the source of that element. In this example, you're going to see every common video format on the Web, starting with WebM (for Opera 10.65+, Firefox 4+, and Chrome), then OGG (for older Opera and older Firefox), and finally MP4 for Safari and Internet Explorer. Following all of that is the standard fallback Flash player:

```
<!DOCTYPE html>
<html lang="en">
  <head>
    <meta charset="utf-8">
  </head>
  <body class="video">
    <video controls autoplay id="video-sample">
      <source src="MVI_1749.webm" type="video/webm">
      <source src="MVI_1749.ogv" type="video/ogg">
      <source src="MVI_1749.mp4" type="video/mp4">
      <object type="application/x-shockwave-flash"
        width="854" height="504"
        data="smallplayer.swf"
        classid="clsid:D27CDB6E-AE6D-11cf-96B8-444553540000">
        <param name="flashvars"
          value="videoURL=MVI_1749.mp4"></param>
        <param name="movie" value="smallplayer.swf"></param>
        <param name="bgcolor" value="#ffffff"></param>
        <param value="true"></param>
        <embed type="application/x-shockwave-flash"
          src="smallplayer.swf"
          bgcolor="#ffffff"
          flashvars="videoURL=MVI_1749.mp4"
          width="854" height="504" ></embed></object>
        <img src="MVI_1749_1.png"
          width="854" height="480" alt="Video">
        <p>Your browser can't play HTML5 video.
          <a href="MVI_1749.mp4">Download it</a> instead.</p>
      </object>
    </video>
  </body>
</html>
```

Theoretically, you can get away with just OGG (it's supported by all versions of Firefox and Opera that support video) and MP4 here, but because there are benefits to serving WebM (quality and size in every browser that supports it and reliability in Chrome), I added the third format to the stack.

This pattern, which was neatly explained and titled Video for Everybody (*http://bit.ly/uw-videoforeverybody*), solves the question of serving video to a good chunk of the population with *just* markup. Sure, it's *ugly* markup with the Flash fallback and multiple `source` elements but it's still just markup, which is nice.

iOS3 Warning
There was a bug in iOS3 which prevented Safari from seeing anything other than the first listed `source`. If, for some reason, iOS3 is a concern for you, you can lead with the MP4 video, which will ensure that it gets a `source` it can handle.

If you're just trying to get video on the page with the default play and pause button, you're basically all set at this point. There are some wrinkles with serving video that you'll learn about in a minute, but getting the video onto the page is sorted at this point. The biggest remaining basic compatibility problem is the loss of a simple, unified JavaScript API. For that, we'll have to turn to the first alternative to a markup-based solution, a JavaScript library built on top of the Video for Everybody pattern called Video.js (*http://www.videojs.com/*).

Video.js

Video.js papers over all of the complexity you've seen so far in this chapter. It also smooths out some of the kinks with compatibility and, most importantly, provides a unified JavaScript API across browsers and platforms. Let's see what it looks like in action.

The first component of note is in the `head` of the document where you insert the Video.js CSS and JavaScript files. That's pretty standard stuff, but you won't get very far without it. After that, there's a small `script` tag where a single Video.js option is set, pointing Video.js to the location of the backup SWF on your server. In the `body` of the page, there's a variation on the Video for Everybody pattern. It's familiar to what you've already seen, but there are a couple of Video.js specific tweaks to notice. The `video` element has two classes for styling, `video-js` and `vjs-default-skin`, and a `data-` attribute (`data-setup`) that in this example contains an empty JavaScript object. Depending on your needs, you might populate this object with several different options (*http://bit.ly/uw-videojs-options*) for instantiating the library.

Inside the `video` element, there are three `source` elements. This is the same as the Video for Everybody pattern. The difference with Video.js is that there's no `object` or `embed` tags for Flash. Thankfully, for the markup at least, Video.js will handle that part if it's needed. This is nice, as it cleans up a big chunk of ugly Flash-centric markup.

The script block is where the real benefit of Video.js comes into play. Video.js provides a unified API, which handles all the differences between the Flash and JavaScript APIs. To kick Video.js off, you pass a reference to your video element to Video.js. This loads Video.js up with the context of the targeted video element. Once you've got that set up, Video.js has a jQuery style ready method, which executes a function as soon as the video is loaded.

The this context of the function argument is the video element itself. I chose to immediately assign this reference to the Video.js enhanced video element to the variable player, for clarity. After that is set up, the Video.js API is basically a mirror of the HTML5 video API, with the one exception of paused. In the HTML5 video API, paused is a property. In Video.js, it needs to be accessed as a method:

```html
<!DOCTYPE html>
<html lang="en">
  <head>
    <meta charset="utf-8">
    <link href="video-js/video-js.css" rel="stylesheet">
    <script src="video-js/video.js"></script>
    <script>
      videojs.options.flash.swf = "video-js/video-js.swf";
    </script>
  </head>
  <body class="video">
    <video class="video-js vjs-default-skin" controls autoplay
      preload="none" id="video-sample" width="854" height="504"
      poster="MVI_1749_1.png"
      data-setup="{}">
      <source src="MVI_1749.webm" type="video/webm">
        <source src="MVI_1749.ogv" type="video/ogg">
        <source src="MVI_1749.mp4" type="video/mp4">
        <img src="MVI_1749_1.png" width="854" height="480"
        alt="Video"  class="vjs-no-js">
        <p class="vjs-no-js">Your browser can't play HTML5
        video. <a href="MVI_1749.mp4">Download it</a>
        instead.</p>
    </video>
    <button id="video-toggle">Pause/Play</button>
    <script>
      videojs("video-sample").ready(function(){
        var player = this,
          toggle = document.getElementById("video-toggle");
        toggle.addEventListener("click", function() {
```

```
    if (player.paused()) {
      player.play();
    } else {
      player.pause();
    }
  });
});
</script>
</body>
</html>
```

This looks like the way the `video` element would look without having to worry about older Internet Explorer. That's a good thing. We *have* added a couple of dependencies with the Video.js script and Video.js CSS. We're also still outputting three separate versions of the same file (although as I mentioned, you could get away with just OGG and MP4). There's also a lot of markup to manage, even without the Flash fallback. So, in short, this is the best cross-browser version of a video embed we've seen so far, and it's *still* a lot to manage. There are several elements, several attributes, Video.js itself, and the looming specter of multiple file formats to consider, just to get a single video into the browser.

Is This a Good Time to Mention Silverlight?

It's not. But I have to mention it at least once, and now is as good a time as any.

If you watch Netflix or Amazon Video (to point out two huge examples) on the PC, you're using a technology called *Silverlight* from Microsoft to stream HD video over the Web. To introduce Silverlight at this point seems like it's just piling on to make your life hell, but it is out there. You wouldn't typically consider it for most video solutions, because not everyone can force a plug-in on their users, but as you can tell by the company, its high-quality streaming is an appealing option for those that can dictate plug-in use.

Have I mentioned the options for video on the Web are confusing?

At this point, even though we've done a decent job of getting cross-browser functionality sorted out, the story isn't over. There are some other factors on the server side to keep in mind when looking at serving video on the Web. Let's take a quick look at the issues as they manifest themselves on the other side of the pipe.

Mime Types and Adaptive Bitrate Streaming

Serving video is a big deal. There are complexities in serving *any-thing* optimally on the Web, but serving video has taken it to an entirely new level. It's complicated, and the penalties for getting it *wrong* can very easily produce a failing or just plain terrible end-user experience. This section won't go into absolute detail, because it's a thorny, evolving subject, but it will go over the issues at play at a really high level so that you'll at least know where to look if you want to upgrade your video experience and keep the end-to-end experience in-house.

Mime types

For starters, video must be served with the proper MIME type. If you don't properly set up your server, your videos will fail to play. This shouldn't be a great hardship, but it is an extra and important step.

For example, if you're using Apache and you've got direct access to your server, it's as simple as adding the following lines to your con-figuration file:

```
AddType video/ogg .ogv
AddType video/mp4 .mp4
AddType video/webm .webm
```

If you're using IIS (*http://bit.ly/uw-iis*) or nginx (*http://bit.ly/uw-nginx*), it's similarly straightforward.

The other part of getting getting video to the browser isn't nearly as straightforward.

Progressive download versus streaming and a performance dead-end for most mortals

Even the perfect format, served to the right player with a correct MIME type is, if it's served over simple HTTP, still just a really big file that the browser needs to download byte by byte. This *progressive download* over simple HTTP can be inefficient because HTTP is built on top of TCP, and TCP is designed to ensure the delivery of all the bytes in a particular message. With video, where smooth playback is far more important to the user experience than the occasional loss of a byte or two (or 1,000 for that matter), that focus on byte delivery can be in-efficient. It's better to use all the available bandwidth to ensure that enough of every frame is available to keep the movie advancing frame by frame in a smooth manner.

With Flash, the standard method to solve this issue was to use a Real-Time Messaging Protocol (RTMP) server. RTMP is a proprietary Adobe technology that works with Flash (another proprietary Adobe technology) to stream video in an efficient manner.

Of course, as the story goes, Flash (and RTMP along with it) were dethroned as the single solution for streaming video with the rise of iOS and the mobile Web in general.

Because the performance argument for streaming video is so strong, Apple provided a separate technology called HTTP Live Streaming (HLS), which provides streaming functionality over regular old HTTP. This technology, now generalized as *adaptive bitrate streaming* because there are other entrants in the market, is a combination of server and client software that detects a user's bandwidth and tweaks the video quality between multiple bitrates and resolutions on the fly. The video stream can be switched midstream to match the client's current connectivity. Compare this to the buffering or playback pause you'll see in progressive download when the bitrate isn't matched by the available download speed. This technology also has the benefit of operating over simple HTTP, with the adaptive bits happening between the client and server at the software level. One major benefit of this is that it's much tougher to block this traffic than it would be to block streaming Flash video, which traveled over a unique port. I commonly had to explain to clients that their video really *did* work, but they just couldn't see it because their IT department was blocking RTMP traffic on port 1935.

HLS is very cool. Unfortunately, it's only supported by iOS and desktop Safari . For other modern browsers (and potentially Apple devices in the future), there's another technology called Dynamic Adaptive Streaming over HTTP (DASH) (*http://dashif.org/*), which fills the same space. It's young, but is gaining momentum rapidly and has support across a good set of newer browsers (Firefox 31+, Chrome 23+, IE 11+, Opera 20+).

So now we've got three separate schemes for streaming video. One works in Flash. One works in iOS and Safari. One is immature and is only supported in the latest versions of a subset of browsers.

It's around this point that I throw in the towel.

Although there *are* resources out there to help you stream audio and video (*http://bit.ly/uw-stream*), including setting up adaptive media sources (*http://bit.ly/uw-adaptive*), the fractured nature of support across the various components of web video, the performance penalties for getting it wrong and the strength and maturity of the online video community make it mighty tempting to just leave it to the pros. You may not come to the same conclusion I have, and you might want to go it alone. But I think it's important that you consider forgoing the granular control you might be used to with other web platform technologies in order to take advantage of the features, functionality, and performance benefits offered by outfits that focus exclusively on video (e.g., YouTube, Vimeo, Brightcove, or Kaltura). Their goal is the same as ours—broad compatibility with whatever the Web can throw at them.

Letting the Pros Handle It

This section will look at a couple of different options available to get your video up on the Web without having to directly manage all of the complexity we've looked at so far. There are many different outlets available for you to get your video on the Web. I recommend YouTube and Vimeo here, because they're free, and you can get up and running quickly. Depending on your specific needs, you might want to stay with one of these or with an entirely different service. In general, the process of uploading and controlling video with one of these services is going to be very similar to what you see here. The biggest differences will really be outside the technical aspects. Things like the customization options available, support options, and bandwidth costs will be a bigger deciding factor for most organizations when compared to the JavaScript API and embed code options.

YouTube

The first example most people think of when they think of online video is probably Google's YouTube service. It's for that reason it's the first option I'm going to show you. Getting videos onto YouTube is as simple as it gets. Assuming you've got an account, all you need to do is hit the Upload button from the YouTube homepage, which brings you to the page shown in Figure 7-2.

The Web Interface Is Not the Only Option
You can also upload directly from the YouTube app on a mobile device or, more importantly for most readers of this book, from the server side using the YouTube API.

Drag a video into the screen or press the Upload button and select a file from your hard drive and your video is on the way to being on the Web just as fast as it can upload (Figure 7-2).

Figure 7-2. Selecting a file to upload on YouTube

From there, you have the option to customize your title and other metadata (Figure 7-3). Make sure everything is good to go and your video is on the Web.

Figure 7-3. Customizing your video on YouTube

To use it on your site, grab the supplied embed code, plug it into your page, and you're done:

```
<!DOCTYPE html>
<html lang="en">
  <head>
    <meta charset="utf-8">
  </head>
  <body class="video">
    <iframe width="560" height="315"
      src="//www.youtube.com/embed/rLaa6q_Cbmc"
      frameborder="0" allowfullscreen></iframe>
  </body>
</html
```

Adding the same simple play/pause interactivity you've seen throughout the chapter is relatively easy using the YouTube JavaScript API. There's one small change to the embed code, namely adding an id to the iframe in order to easily bind events to it with JavaScript. Following that, there's a script tag, which includes the iframe API JavaScript file from YouTube. The script that runs the interaction should be familiar enough at this point. The one YouTube specific wrinkle that really needs some explanation is the onYouTubeIframeAPIReady function. This function gets called automatically when the iframe API JavaScript file is loaded. Inside the function body, you set a player variable with a reference to the id of the iframe embedded in the page earlier. The second argument, here an empty object, can be populated with other properties. These potential options are especially useful if you're loading a player dynamically, because you can set the player's width, height, YouTube video ID (to load a video dynamically), events, as well as a slew of other player variables (*http://bit.ly/uw-ytplayers*). The rest of the javaScript mirrors the code you've seen in both the pure JavaScript and Video.JS examples with slightly more verbose method names and properties. The one important difference is the presence of the more powerful `player.getPlayerState()` method in place of the simple `paused` property or `paused()` method you saw in the other examples. Here you're checking for two separate states of the player, `paused` and `video cued`. The full list of states and associated integer codes are listed in Table 7-1.

Table 7-1. YouTube video states

code	status
-1	unstarted
0	ended
1	playing
2	paused
3	buffering
5	video cued

The source of the example follows:

```
<!DOCTYPE html>
<html lang="en">
  <head>
    <meta charset="utf-8">
  </head>
  <body class="video">
    <iframe id="player" width="560" height="315"
      src="//www.youtube.com/embed/rLaa6q_Cbmc?enablejsapi=1"
      frameborder="0" allowfullscreen></iframe>
    <p><button id="video-toggle">Pause/Play</button></p>
    <script src="//www.youtube.com/iframe_api"></script>
    <script>
      var player;
      function onYouTubeIframeAPIReady() {
        player = new YT.Player('player', {});
      }
      toggle = document.getElementById("video-toggle");
      toggle.addEventListener("click", function() {
        if (player.getPlayerState() === 2
            || player.getPlayerState() === 5 ) {
          player.playVideo();
```

```
      } else {
        player.pauseVideo();
      }
    });
  </script>
  </body>
</html>
```

All in all, this is a straightforward implementation with probably hundreds (thousands?) of engineers backing it up on the YouTube side. Without having to know *anything* about compression, adaptive bitrate streaming, containers, or codecs, you can get up and running with video on the Web in just a few minutes. The downside of YouTube is that it's ad driven and, at the end of the day, is *YouTube*. Depending on your needs, an ad supported, mass-market platform might not be right for you. If it is, it's easy to get started, has a pretty powerful API on both the server and client side, and is supported by Google, so it's got the power of the Internet giant behind it.

If YouTube is not your thing, there are plenty of other options. Although we can't look at them all in this slim volume, we can take a look at one that skips the ads, adds options for paid enhancements, and presents slightly hipper packaging: Vimeo.

Vimeo

Using Vimeo (*https://vimeo.com/*) follows a similar pattern to that of YouTube. Basically, you hit Vimeo, click the Upload button, and you're presented with a simple page to start the upload process (Figure 7-4).

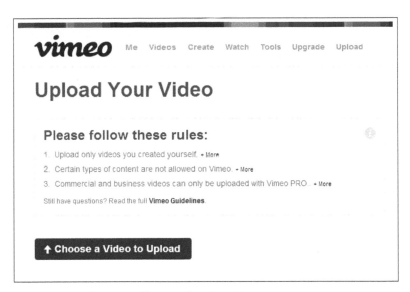

Figure 7-4. Selecting a file to upload on Vimeo

From there, just like YouTube, you can customize your title and other metadata, and then you're ready to share your video with the world (Figure 7-5). One difference with Vimeo is that it sometimes takes longer for your video to get on the Web as a free user. You're in a compression/conversion queue with the rest of the riffraff. Unless you're publishing breaking news, this isn't all that much of a big deal, but it's something to note in advance, if you're looking to Vimeo as an alternative to YouTube for your video hosting.

Figure 7-5. Customizing your video on Vimeo

To use it on your own site, grab the embed code (once again a single line iframe) and paste it into the body of your page:

```
<!DOCTYPE html>
<html lang="en">
  <head>
    <meta charset="utf-8">
  </head>
  <body class="video">
    <iframe src="//player.vimeo.com/video/103677495"
      width="500" height="281" frameborder="0"
      webkitallowfullscreen mozallowfullscreen
      allowfullscreen></iframe>
  </body>
</html>
```

Our interactivity example is also available using the Vimeo API. It should be noted that, although I like the *look and feel* of Vimeo and the Vimeo player, the API and API documentation aren't at the same level as YouTube.

As you can see, it's a little bit more code to get the same interactivity and what *is* there isn't as straightforward. That said, it gets the job done and that might be all that matters if Vimeo as a whole works for you.

In the code, the first piece to note are some small tweaks to the URL of the embedded movie. The first change is the addition of `?api=1` to the URL. This argument gets the player ready to listen to API calls from your JavaScript. Then, in an only partially documented wrinkle, you need to pass the `player_id` of the embedded `iframe` to the player. Without it, none of the API calls will work as expected. This is mentioned in the documentation, but only in reference to multiple players on the page. Even with only one player, if you're going to reference it by `id`, I've found you need this argument appended to the player URL for anything to work. Following that, you'll need to add the Vimeo API JavaScript file to the document.

In case you're wondering, I *haven't* researched why it's called Froogaloop.

The script block itself is more complicated than any example we've seen before. It's not completely horrendous, just different. To kick things off, you need to pass a reference to the embedded `iframe` to the Froogaloop function `$f`. At this point, the `player` variable is loaded with the Vimeo API. Then you create a variable `paused`, which you're going to use to track the state of the player. There *is* a Vimeo API method `paused`, but the way the Vimeo API works makes using that built-in API method awkward. The Vimeo API uses `postmessage` to handle messaging between the `iframe`, the `browser`, and the `contain ing` page. Because `postmessage` relies on callback functions to do some of its work, and the Vimeo API hews pretty strictly to that pattern, the `paused` method isn't quite as easy to use as the `paused` properties and methods that we've seen. To access the value of the `paused` API call, you actually need to pass in a second function, which would then act on the information provided by the API. It doesn't just return a Boolean directly to the calling scope. It only returns the Boolean to the callback function. So, instead of using the awkward API method, it's easier to just track this variable manually by binding methods against the built-in `pause`, `finish`, and `playProgress` events. Following that bit of nonsense, the second wrinkle is the *generally* awkward API design. Instead of the `player.APITMETHOD()` you might expect, the Vimeo API methods are passed in as string arguments to the `play er.api` method. This is actually pretty weird. It's not a very common

JavaScript API design (I think I've seen a couple of jQuery plug-ins that did this but not many), so it might be a little confusing if you're not aware of it in advance. With that sorted, the rest of the pattern is similar to the examples you've seen throughout this chapter with play and pause methods used to control the player:

```html
<!DOCTYPE html>
<html lang="en">
  <head>
    <meta charset="utf-8">
  </head>
  <body class="video">
    <iframe id="player"
     src=
"//player.vimeo.com/video/103677495?api=1&amp;player_id=player"
        width="500" height="281" frameborder="0"
        webkitallowfullscreen mozallowfullscreen
        allowfullscreen></iframe>
    <p><button id="video-toggle">Pause/Play</button></p>
    <script src="//f.vimeocdn.com/js/froogaloop2.min.js">
    </script>
    <script>
      var player = $f(document.getElementById("player"));
      var paused=true;
      var toggle = document.getElementById("video-toggle");
      player.addEvent('ready', function() {
        player.addEvent('pause', function() {
          paused=true;
        });
        player.addEvent('finish', function() {
          paused=true;
        });
        player.addEvent('playProgress', function() {
          paused=false;
        });
      });
      toggle.addEventListener("click", function() {
        if (paused) {
          player.api("play");
        } else {
          player.api("pause");
        }
      });
    </script>
  </body>
</html>
```

It should be pointed out that if the Froogaloop interface to the API isn't to your liking, and it probably won't be if you're anything like me, you can use postmessage directly to control the player. Vimeo documents this as well as Froogaloop on their API documentation. It's everything else that Vimeo brings that makes it worth taking a a look at, so working through the kinks of communication between your page and their player might be a small hurdle, depending on your needs.

Make the Best of a Complicated Situation

In this chapter, you've seen what can happen when good specifications go bad once they hit the mean streets. From the clear beginnings of the video element as a replacement for plug-in-based video on the Web to today's nasty mosaic of options to sort through in order to get video on the Web, we're looking at a present where a modern Web standards-based solution isn't necessarily better than what came before. Although having to use a proprietary technology like Flash isn't part of the ideal Web I really want, I also want a Web that's easy to manage from a workflow perspective and doesn't add multiple layers of complexity to my life just to get my job done. There's hope on the horizon in the form of the HTML video element, DASH, and MP4/h. 264 (or better yet, the unlikely adoption of a patent-free alternative), but that simple future remains out of reach. Until that magical time, you've got to look long and hard at your video solution, keeping all options on the table. Whether you decide to go it alone or if you decide to leverage one of the many third parties, this is one situation where it's best to just hold your nose and make decisions based on what's best for your users, rather than what might be the best possible solutions from a pure web standards perspective.

More importantly, in the context of this book at least, the overall complexity of video reinforces the idea that no matter what the intentions are of the standards bodies, the real world can throw a spanner in the works really quickly. When it does and market forces or the commercial interests of browser vendors get in the way, it's better to acknowledge that issue early on and move ahead with the best practical solution. Being a champion for web standards is a great thing, as long as it's not at the expense of your end users.

CHAPTER 8

The Web We Want

> The Web as I envisaged it, we have not seen it yet.
> The future is still so much bigger than the past.
>
> — Tim Berners-Lee

In this book, I've poked around some places where the Web is a strange beast. As the title of the book will tell you, I've done so to help you manage the Web's uncertainty. I've also done so in order to help the Web grow stronger. The more light we shine on the areas of the Open Web Platform that don't work, the better prepared we'll be as we build the Web moving forward. Sure, we may never be able to get a patent-free standard for web video, but that just gives us more motivation to make sure the Web comes out on top the next time a fight breaks out between the Web and entrenched commercial interests. We've got to expose the places where the process has fallen apart or fallen prey to unsavory interests in order to make sure we don't make those same mistakes the next time.

This is how we continue to grow the Web and how we strengthen the web platform.

I *truly* believe in the quote that opens this chapter. The future of the Web is much bigger than the past. How much bigger comes down to people like you and me. With the changes we're witnessing, there's never been a better time to dive in and try to make a difference.

This chapter will look at where we've been in this book and some key points to take away as we spread off to the four corners of the globe to make the Web a better place for more people, on more devices, and in more browsers.

Things Can Get Better (But They Do Occasionally Get Worse)

This section will present a slightly unique twist on one of the standard tech book final chapter constructs—*reviewing what you've learned*. I'm interested in looking forward in this last chapter, so I'm not going to recap everything I've talked about so far in detail. Instead, I'm going to share anecdotes that do reference previous chapter topics. These will reinforce just how much is happening on the ground today and how we can all work together to make sure things get better as we move the Web forward.

You see, three of the chapter topics have changed *significantly* from a technical or support perspective since I first conceived of this book. These changes have forced me to change my take on each topic and adjust my recommendations accordingly. This has happened throughout the process of writing this book. It happened once during the planning stage, once in mid-chapter, and once after a chapter had been written. Three major changes in less than a year and a half. Two of these were positive changes (one more than the other). One was decidedly negative.

Firefox Announced Support for h.264

Right when I was kicking off this project, it was announced that Mozilla had found a way (through a partnership with Cisco) to provide support for h.264 video in the Firefox browser. Before this announcement, the video situation on the Web was even uglier than it is now, with two sides much more evenly divided across the patent-friendly and patent-free camps. Web users and web developers were caught in the middle.

As you've learned, h.264 support in Firefox isn't a salve for everything wrong with video on the Web, but it definitely lowered the overall tension level and proved that even when things look hopeless (as it did in regards to Firefox supporting h.264), things can change rapidly.

The downside to that is that a patent-free alternative to h.264 would be better for the Web, and Firefox standing its ground would have strengthened the side of the good guys. Of course, it would have hurt Firefox in some ways, and, to be honest, getting Apple and Microsoft to walk away from the h.264 specification would have been a longshot, as they're owners of some of the patents administered by MPEG LA (*http://bit.ly/uw-mpegla*) (the patent pool that administers the licenses for h.264). But it was still one of those times that Firefox proved they were fighting for the Open Web in a way that the other browser vendors can't.

So, in some ways, Cisco coming through was good for the Web in terms of general compatibility, but part of me wishes that Firefox was still holding out for a better open solution. Although I'm pragmatic enough to use what's available, the core technologies we're building the Web upon shouldn't be controlled by commercial interests. In the case of video, we're all beholden at one level or another to MPEG LA. That stinks.

Picture Comes Back from the Dead

In the *middle* of writing the already tricky chapter on responsive images, the `picture` element came all the way back from the dead and made it into the specification and Chrome 38, the latest production version of Chrome.

It had been coming for a while so I only had to rewrite a bit of what I was working on, and, overall, I was happy about this change. Even though I'm not a huge fan of the markup, having this option available for the most complicated responsive image use cases is a big deal. It's also the single best, recent example of web developers, browser vendors, and the folks writing the specifications working together in order to solve a real-world problem. I would rather that it hadn't taken four years, but it did happen and that's the important thing.

The tireless work on this solution with hands-on involvement from many camps should serve as a guiding example of the attitude we all need to take going forward. If something is broken, we need to fix it, and we need to work together to get the best solution possible into the browser. We also can't give up just because we hear "no" from the browser vendors or the standards bodies. In many ways, the final push for the return of `picture` was spurred on by the dismissive reaction by a Safari developer to an alternative to `picture` called `src-n` (he called it "a grotesque perversion of the HTML language"). The community heard "no" one last time and realized that *something* needed to get done.

And then it did.

Pointer Events Might Be Dead

As you've read in the chapter on user input, the Pointer Events specification, proposed by Microsoft, favored by Firefox and adopted by the W3C, is up in the air because Chrome isn't sure whether or not they are going to support it. This was announced *after* I finished the chapter on user input. I found out via Twitter that Chrome was going to pull planned support for Pointer Events (*http://bit.ly/uw-chr-pointer-support*) and felt about as deflated as I've ever felt about a web standards topic. For one thing, I like Pointer Events. I'm not sharing them as the way of the future just to be hip and share the new stuff. I really like them. Secondly, Google's proposed alternative, "incrementally extending our existing input APIs" doesn't really offer much of a salve to the wound of two wasted years looking for this specification to get off the ground and into browsers.

Maybe, like the door on `picture` being reopened and bursting through to get into the specification, the already specified Pointer Events' work will come back from the dead and make it into Chrome and the rest of modern browsers. The Chrome team are listening to feedback, so hopefully that's just what's going to happen. (*http://bit.ly/uw-chrome-pointer*)

We shall see.

I Knew Something Like This Would Happen

When I started writing a book about the uncertain nature of the modern Web, I knew that there would be flux in the very topics I chose to write about. I just didn't expect it to touch 60% of the purely technical chapters in significant ways.

And this talk of change ignores all of the other, environmental things that are happening all the time. We've got fewer users of IE6 and Android 2.3, for example. You still have to be aware of them, but we're getting closer (slowly) to the day where they're gone. Things are improving—we just need to be active and help the process along as best we can while still trying to reach as many folks as we can.

Let's Push Things Forward

To me, the Web remains a remarkable platform with unparalleled reach, tons of content, a rich history of innovation, and a knack for doing crazy things with whatever is at hand. The things that people have been able to do with the Web in the first 20 years, especially in the dark ages when the tools were horrible, are remarkable. I believe in the Web like crazy and think that if we move forward with the same energy and genius we've shown over the past 20 years, the next 20 years will be even greater. We just need to embrace the Web for being the Web, build *for the Web* and ensure that the foundation the Web is built on is as strong as possible.

How do we do that? I've talked about the technical components throughout the book. Providing widely accessible sites and applications is an important component of keeping the Web healthy. People have to be happy with the Web today if we have any chance of keeping them on it in the future. There are other, not strictly technical components that I think are just as important.

I'm going to leave you with those.

A Web Built By Developers, Browser Vendors, and Standards Bodies

Web developers have to be better at influencing the standards process. You've learned about successes in this book. The responsive image solutions we have now are all down to a large degree to web developer advocacy. It didn't come up much in this book, but, for all its controversies, the TC39 group that writes the ECMAScript (commonly known as JavaScript) specification is populated by working developers who have strong voices. They have helped steer the development of the specification in ways that will make our lives better for years to come.

The thing is, we can do better. As of this writing, and after many years of discussion, we still don't have a script-loading and dependency solution that everyone can live with. I'm not sure if we even have a set of agreed-upon requirements and use cases. We still have the mess of dealing with user input. We're still scrambling in 15 different directions to get video into the browser.

We can solve these problems. We just need to make sure that the browser vendors and specification authors really understand what we're trying to do, and we need to pressure them when they go astray.

It may not seem like it at times, but we're all on the same side. We need to trust in the process and in one another. But that trust has to come along with a commitment from the web developer community that we're going to help them along the way with constructive feedback and a desire to roll up our sleeves and get to work (*http://responsiveim ages.org/*). We're getting way better at this, but we can do more.

For a concrete example that's also highly topical for this book, the push to resuscitate Chrome's intent to implement Pointer Events has been led by developers. Stars and comments on the Chromium issue (*http:// bit.ly/uw-chrome-pointer*) have ballooned since they marked it as a "won't fix," so hopefully steady pressure from the developer community will get them to change their mind.

Regardless of the end result of that push, there are a couple of lessons to take from this. The first is, we should have gotten involved earlier. I am guilty of this one myself. As I mentioned, I'm a fan of Pointer Events, and I've been on the issue several times in the course of writing this book. I didn't start it or comment on it until they marked it "won't fix." I am, in other words, a big dummy. The second is, our voices matter, and we need to raise them. If there's something that matters to you, like Mat Marquis' championing of responsive images, then you should make that interest known. Individuals can directly influence the growth and transformation of the Web. It's a great opportunity. It's not every day you can work on something that will ripple through and affect a billion people. The Web offers that.

There are many ways to get involved. From offering feedback on specifications, to writing polyfills, to testing browser implementations of new web features, all the way to getting down to the business of writing proposals for new web features and functionality, the possibilities are pretty much endless if you've got the interest and will to see the process through to the end.

A Web That Is Fast, Widely Available, and Reliable

To me, beyond the basic value proposition (are you providing cool information or a great service?), if you're building a website or application that is fast, widely available, and reliable, you're more than half-way there. If there's one thread that runs throughout the examples you've seen so far, it's that there's always a thought given to when things go horribly awry. If you accept that things will be bonkers from time to time and that someone might try to visit your site on Opera Mini running on a Micromax phone in the middle of the swirling chaos of the Chandni Chowk market in Delhi (Figure 8-1) you can start to anticipate the kind of problems your users might see. Does that guy care whether or not you've got high DPI images for your hero image or if you've got drop shadows on all your menus? Not really. Chances are pretty good he wants to access your site, retrieve his information, and get back to his business.

Figure 8-1. Chandni Chowk as seen from the Jama Masjid mosque

The dirty truth of the Web is that desire to get in, get out, and get on with life is true for people with good computers and strong connections. A biochemist in Peoria might be impressed by the excellent fit and finish of your site, but if your site takes 45 seconds to load even over her research lab's broadband connection, she might never get to see it because she will have already hit her back button or simply closed the tab.

I'm all for awesome experiences, and there are plenty of places where the experience can be the whole purpose of a site. (*http://www.ro.me/*) That kind of work is vital to ensure that the techniques we're using stay fresh and that we really pound on new technologies to know where they break.

That said, the power of the Web is that it's universal. There's no app store. Everything is available to everyone, or at least it should be. We've got to strive to make that the default for the way that we build for the Web. We should ensure that even in the worst circumstances, something useful is there for the user. We should ensure that even in the best circumstances, we focus our attention on serving our user's needs and not our own vanity.

A Web Where There's Nothing to Win

I'm happy to change my mind if I'm presented with new evidence or if I simply see things in a new light. One of the biggest turnabouts I've had recently is my take on the "us versus them" approach many web developers take toward the mobile app space. For many web developers (and me up until about two years ago), the question of native versus mobile Web is an existential crisis and is one that can only be solved by replicating the app experience on the mobile Web. We have to "beat them" with better experiences, so we need to amp up the technical toolbox to match them tit for tat. This is one of the reasons we get so much attention focused on the hottest, hippest technology in demos and why so much time is spent on the WHATWG discussing how we get access to the same device-style APIs that native app developers get.

The thing is, it's not a zero-sum game. Just like TV and movies can all coexist, the Web and native app space can also coexist and even thrive. The Web's ubiquity, platform independence, and freedom to experiment can't be matched inside the walled gardens of the App Store and Google Play. Firing up an idea for the Web and seeing how it goes can happen as fast as your fingers can type and as fast as you can spin up a web server. There's no approval process, and there's no Apple or Google standing over your shoulder making sure you don't break some arbitrary rule—or with a paw out waiting for a cut.

There's also no ceiling on how big you can get. Well, with the exception of the scale of the Web itself, but that's pretty big (and includes all of the devices running Android, iOS, Windows Phone, and whatever other OS you want to throw at it).

Not too shabby.

The Web, if we do it right, is there for everybody as soon as they fire up a web browser and unlike trying to catch lighting in a bottle to simply get noticed in an Apple or Google-shaped sandbox, building for the Web means you're only limited by what you want to do and whom you want to reach.

So, for one example that's taken a lot of people's time, don't get bent out of shape if people are spending a lot of time playing games on their smartphones. Do you stress out about the XBox? No? Then don't worry about people playing games on their smartphones. If you're interested in the Web as a medium for games, then run with it. There's lots of opportunity there, but don't go into game dev on the Web just to compete with smartphones. The Web didn't get to where it is by trying to replicate one-to-one the features and functionality of other media. It did its own thing and brought over features when they made sense for the Web. When they came over, they changed to suit the Web. The limitations of the web platform have always been something we've had to work around, and those limitations have helped keep web developers creative. We can improve the fundamentals, but that ability to bend things to the Web's will is still a skill we ought to keep.

The Web We Want Starts with Us

I've written a couple of books before this one, including a big doorstop introduction to the breadth of the web platform. Those were pretty straightforward. If you're showing someone how to build a menu using a `nav` element and a `ul`, you just build out the menu and explain how it all works. There's also usually pretty good documentation for whatever you happen to be writing about, so if you're stumped, you can always hit the Web or another book to figure out what's going on. This book has been different. My main goal isn't to to show you how to implement different features. Sure, I hope you understand `picture` at this point, and I really hope you have a better sense of how user input works on the modern Web, but I've really been trying to get you to think about the way you approach building for the Web. I don't do all of the things I want to do on every site, so I don't expect anyone else to take everything to heart. What I do hope is that you'll questions your assumptions and when you're planning your site or app, you will try to include rather than exclude users whenever possible. I also hope that you'll take the opportunity to help strengthen the Web as a whole by helping out in the standards process in whatever way you can.

By building the best sites we can and trying to reach the most people we can with the best possible experience across a variety of devices, we'll be one step closer to fulfilling the universal promise of the Web.

How cool is that?

Index

We'd like to hear your suggestions for improving our indexes. Send email to index@oreilly.com.

G

Garrett, Jesse James, 20
Gecko (layout engine), 8
gestural interfaces, 25
gestures, 132
    (see also touch-related topics)
    Internet Explorer browsers that
        recognize, 136
GIFs, 167
GitHub.com, keyboard shortcuts on,
    53
Google
    emulators offered through An-
        droid SDK, 45
    WeP image format, 165
Google Android (see Android brows-
    er; Android OS)
Google Chrome (see Chrome)
Graphic Interchange Format (GIF),
    167
Guardian, The, RWD news site, 110

H

h.264 video codec, 197
    Firefox support of, 216
HCIs (see human/computer inter-
    faces)
Heritage Auctions website, mobile
    and desktop areas, 121
HLS (HTTP Live Streaming), 203
hover events, not relying too heavily
    on, 142, 143
hover-capable devices, 25, 134
HTML
    early misperception of, 16
    standards development today,
        tracking, 21
    user agents, past and future, sup-
        porting, 57
HTML 4.0, 14
HTML5, 19, 21
    cross-browser polyfills in Modern-
        izr, 84
    document outline, viewing, 53
    monitoring developments in, 66
    sectioning elements, 122
    track element, 193

video element, 191, 192–196
HTML5 Boilerplate project, 77
HTML5Shiv, 74
    inlining, 76
    using directly, 75
HTTP Live Streaming (HLS), 203
Huawei, 46
Huffington Post, mobile and desktop
    URLs, 113
human/computer interfaces (HCIs),
    25

I

icon fonts, 58
    Modernizr test for, 93
IE Mobile, 11
    mobile browser market share, 12
images
    connections speeds and, 24
    on the Web, complex world of,
        159–189
        choosing sizes/images at differ-
           ent breakpoints, 164
        embracing SVG, 182–186
        images should be easy, 165
        on the server side, 186
        optimizing images for the Web,
           165–170
        practical developers guide,
           186–188
        responsive images, 170–181
        serving correct format, 165
        serving correct image for mul-
           tiple pixel ratio devices, 164
        serving correctly sized images
           to multiple resolutions, 164
        serving smallest possible file
           size, 163
        solutions to complexity, 188
        taking advantage of browser
           preloader, 163
    text alternatives for, display in dif-
        ferent browsers, 50
img element
    sizes attribute, 173
    srcset attribute, 172, 178
immersive desktop experiences, 103

Lenovo, 46
links, 55
    alternate rel attribute and associated media query, 115
    canonical, 114
    difficulty of getting users to follow, 113
    management of, dedicated mobile experience, 107
localStorage, 118
long running script errors, 60
lossy compression, 166

M

Mac operating systems, 58
    testing against, 44
maintenance
    dedicated moblile experience applications and, 107
    RWD applications, 104
media queries, 124
    in link element, rel attribute, 115
    testing with Modernizr.mq, 87
Meyer, Eric, 17
Microsoft
    .Net MVC framework, 101
    account sign-up form, inline validation and contextual help, 56
    Kinect, 26
    Silverlight, 201
Microsoft monoculture, 2, 5
MIME types, video, 202
mistakes, helping users to avoid and correct, 56
mobile devices
    browsers and their market shares, 12
    developing for predominantly mobile market, 39
    human/computer interface (HCI) revolution, 25
    inferring incorrectly from window object property, 139
    iPhone as dominant platform, 59
    testing against mobile browsers, 43
    text alternatives for non-text content, 50

trifecta of mobile user antagonism, 120
Mobile First, 100, 101
mobile Web, 6
mobile website design, 96
    (see also responsive web design)
    approaches other than RWD, 100
        dedicated mobile experience, 100
        Mobile First, 101
        RESS, 102
    being fluid, designing for your design, 122
    choosing a development path, 102
    choosing architecture best for your project, 110
    dedicated mobile experience
        benefits of, 106
        downsides of, 107
    escape from mobile version, always offering, 119
    how Alexa top 10 sites handle mobile devices, 108
    redirects, options for, 115
        more complicated queries, 118
Model View Controller (MVC), frontend libraries and frameworks, 64
Modernizr, 69
    additional methods, 86
        Modernizr.mq, 87
        Modernizr.prefix, 86
    common feature tests and associated polyfills, 90
    customizing, 80
    Emoji rendering support, testing for, 72
    HTML5 cross-browser polyfills, 84
    load utility, being pulled from core build, 84
    touch capabilities tests, 135
    undetectable features, dealing with, 88
    using, 73
        and not using, 74
        feature detection with, 77
        modernizing old Internet Explorer, 73
        what it does and doesn't do, 73

VML (Vector Markup Language), 39

W

W3C (World Wide Web Consortium), 14
  Pointer Events standardization, 156
W3C Workshop on Web Applications and Compound Documents, 17
WAI-ARIA roles, HTML5 sectioning elements, 122
web application development
  choosing a development path, factors in, 102
  choosing architecture best for your project, 110
  online resources, xiii
web applications
  flexibility, limited with RWD, 106
  heightened flexibility with dedicated mobile experience, 106
  lower complexity in RWD applications, 105
  switching from mobile to desktop versions, 119
Web Apps 1.0, 19
Web as development platform, x
Web Content Accessibility Guidelines 2.0 Appendix B, 50
Web Controls 1.0, 19
web developers
  need for greater influence on standards process, 219
  spreading your wings and questioning your assumptions, 67
  stack biases, losing, 63–65
  technology biases, losing, 58–63
Web Forms 2.0, 19
Web Hypertext Application Technology Working Group (WHATWG), 17
  monitoring HTML5 developments from, 66
web page for this book, xvi
web platform, 2
  (see also Open Web Platform)

support matrices for many features, 42
Web Standards Project (WaSP), 17
web storage specification, 118
Web, future of, 215
  fast, widely avalable, and reliable Web, 220
  Firefox support for h.264, 216
  foundations built by developers, browser vendors, and standards bodies, 219
  picture element, rebirth of, 217
  possible death of Pointer events, 218
  pushing things forward, 218
  things can get better, 216
  Web we want starts with us, 223
  Web with nothing to win, 222
WebKit-based browsers, 8
  jQuery patches and fixes for, 64
  SquirrelFish Extreme/Nitro JavaScript engine, 9
  text alternative for broken images, 50
  UC Browser, 11
WebM/VP8 video container/codec, 197
WebP images, 165, 168
  prepping the files, 179
websites, looking the same on every browser, 47
WHATWG (Web Hypertext Application Technology Working Group), 17
  monitoring HTML5 developments from, 66
Wikipedia, handling of mobile devices, 108
window.ontouchstart, 135, 138
window.sessionStorage, 115
Windows systems
  Firefox and Chrome on Windows 8, touch test results, 135
  market share, 59
  testing against, 44
  Windows 8 laptop, 25, 131
  Windows XP in China, 38

About the Author

Rob Larsen has spent 13 years building websites and applications for some of the world's biggest brands. He applied that experience to teaching a broad audience in *Beginning HTML and CSS*.

Colophon

The animal on the cover of *The Uncertain Web* is the Oriental flying gurnard (*Dactyloptena orientalis*). This bottom-dwelling saltwater fish takes its name from the Old French word "gurnard," meaning to grunt; this refers to a distinctive croaking sound it makes when taken out of the water, produced by a muscle that thumps against its swim bladder. Other names include sea robin and helmet gurnard, an allusion to its wide, square head.

Found in the Indo-Pacific region, from East Africa to Polynesia, Australia, and New Zealand, flying gurnard typically inhabit shallow waters, including estuaries, coastal bays, and sandy areas. Most measure between 20 and 40 centimeters (8 and 16 inches) in length, with a brownish-colored body that tapers from head to tail.

Its most remarkable feature is its massive rounded pectoral fins, which resemble wings. They are usually held against the body, but when threatened, the fish spreads them out to the side, causing it to appear much larger to its enemies. The fins are tinged with bright blue markings and sport dark spots that resemble eyes, which serve to further confuse potential predators such as sea breams and mackerel.

In spite of its name, the flying gurnard is not actually capable of flying. Rather, it uses its pelvic fins to "walk" along the ocean floor in search of food. Its diet includes bivalves, crustaceans, and small, bony fish.

Many of the animals on O'Reilly covers are endangered; all of them are important to the world. To learn more about how you can help, go to animals.oreilly.com.

The cover image is from loose plates (original source unknown). The cover fonts are URW Typewriter and Guardian Sans. The text font is Adobe Minion Pro; the heading font is Adobe Myriad Condensed; and the code font is Dalton Maag's Ubuntu Mono.

Get even more for your money.

Join the O'Reilly Community, and register the O'Reilly books you own. It's free, and you'll get:

- $4.99 ebook upgrade offer
- 40% upgrade offer on O'Reilly print books
- Membership discounts on books and events
- Free lifetime updates to ebooks and videos
- Multiple ebook formats, DRM FREE
- Participation in the O'Reilly community
- Newsletters
- Account management
- 100% Satisfaction Guarantee

Signing up is easy:

1. Go to: oreilly.com/go/register
2. Create an O'Reilly login.
3. Provide your address.
4. Register your books.

Note: English-language books only

To order books online:
oreilly.com/store

For questions about products or an order:
orders@oreilly.com

To sign up to get topic-specific email announcements and/or news about upcoming books, conferences, special offers, and new technologies:
elists@oreilly.com

For technical questions about book content:
booktech@oreilly.com

To submit new book proposals to our editors:
proposals@oreilly.com

O'Reilly books are available in multiple DRM-free ebook formats. For more information:
oreilly.com/ebooks

Milton Keynes UK
Ingram Content Group UK Ltd.
UKHW050944270324
440141UK00009B/84